Renewal

Grace and Redemption in the Story of Ruth

Jerome Gay, Jr.

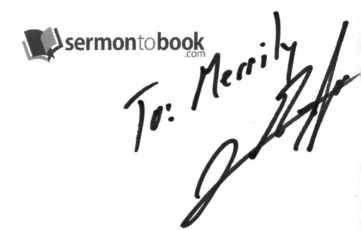

Sermon To Book
www.sermontobook.com

Renewal / Jerome Gay, Jr.
ISBN-13: 978-1-945793-26-4
ISBN-10: 1-945793-26-0

"Immensely biblical, yet refreshingly practical—Pastor Jerome Gay has outfitted readers with much-needed confidence for the journey that lies ahead. If you've ever wondered if God really loves you, or found yourself sinking in swamps of shame, your reservoirs of hope will be renewed once you finish this much-needed book!"

—**Bryan Loritts, Lead Pastor of Abundant Life and author of *Saving the Saved***

"A delightful treatment of one of the Bible's most beautiful stories. Pastor Jerome's insight is both penetrating and practical, and the beauty of the gospel shines forth from every chapter. I'll be glad to have this resource sitting on my shelf for use both personally and pastorally. This is the kind of book that could only come from someone who faithfully walks with God and alongside real people, a message of hope arising from a man who has devoted his life to helping hurting people."

—**Pastor JD Greear of The Summit Church, author of *Gospel, Stop Asking Jesus into Your Heart*, and *Gaining by Losing***

"Jerome is a modern-day theologian.... His uncanny savvy to unearth the ancient depths of the biblical text as well as nuance it for our day is genius. I'm so glad to have his voice that I have heard for almost a decade, that I have heard through his journey, now written. Take this work and apply it to areas of your life where you are trusting God to redeem."

—**Eric Mason, Pastor of Epiphany Fellowship, President of Thriving, and author of *Manhood Restored***

"Jerome Gay, Jr., has a way of making timeless truths simple and relatable. In his book *Renewal*, he captures the beauty of the gospel in the story of Ruth, while giving his readers practical ways to apply the gospel daily. In whatever season you may be in your life, this book will challenge and inspire you to live with a renewed perspective on every aspect of life. *Renewal* is a gospel-centered, grace-saturated book that I highly recommend for anyone, and it's a great read for individuals and entire churches. If you plan on studying or teaching the book of Ruth, this is a book that must be on your shelf."

—**Derwin Gray, Pastor of Transformation Church and author of *HD Leader***

To Crystal — You renewed my outlook on life the moment I met you, and I'm grateful to God for your love and the fact that I get to call you my wife. You mean the world to me, and I love you.

To Jamari and Jordan — I don't deserve to be your dad. You two are reminders of how gracious God has been to me, and I love both of you. This is for you—and remember, nothing is too hard for God.

To my mom and my brother — You have been my support, and I love you for being there for me and wanting nothing but the best for me.

To Vision Church — You are the best group of people I know, and I couldn't ask for a better group of people to serve. You are my family, and I love you all.

CONTENTS

A Timeless Story of Love

The Bible conveys God's Word to us through numerous types of writing, from history and law to poetry and prophecy to letters and laws.

Ultimately, however, the whole of the Bible is a love story—the story of God's love for humanity.

So, it makes perfect sense that at least one book of the Bible would be, in fact, a romantic story of finding love.

Hence, we find the book of Ruth.

Beyond being a tale of unlikely love, however, the ancient story of Ruth has much to say to believers and non-believers today.

The book of Ruth is set in the Middle East approximately 1,100 years before Christ walked this earth. The heroine was a foreign woman from the wrong side of the tracks, from a race of people whom God's chosen people, the Israelites, despised. Her love interest was a good man, but unlike in the typical chick flick, he was old enough to be her father.

Yet if you thought this old Bible story, set in a distant culture, would have little relevance to the twenty-first-century dating scene, think again!

It turns out that while cultures and social structures change, human nature does not. As the poet and wisdom writer Solomon said, "Nothing under the sun is truly new" (Ecclesiastes 1:9). Thus, we can appreciate the wisdom from a story of old. Even amid vastly different cultures, our human eccentricities remain distinctly familiar.

We ought to read the book of Ruth as a story of grace, of undeserved favor poured out on both Jews and Gentiles (non-Jews). In the four short chapters of this book of Scripture, we find disappointment and despair, bitterness and regret—emotions common to us all. But we also witness a story of hope, encouragement, and renewed perspectives, all played out on the canvas of Old Testament Palestine.

Though the historical characters in this story experience a discouraging start, their shortcomings and challenges show us how God renews and redeems. We will discover how God can redeem the effects of bad decision-making.

We must realize that even if we've made a mistake— or a slew of them—there's grace for us. We can start over. We can make a U-turn.

The magnificent reality is that because of the grace extended to us by Christ, none of our failures is irrevocable. Some people want us to believe there's no turning back after making a bad decision. But if we are in Christ, even our failures can be redeemed.

God still has a plan and a purpose for us. *In Christ, there is always a do-over.* But without Him, we are left to fend for ourselves when everything falls apart.

In this story, we meet the widow Naomi and her family, including her foreign daughter-in-law Ruth, who wanted to accompany her mother-in-law home to the land of the Israelites. We will also meet Boaz, whom Ruth eventually marries. The focus of the story is redemption, and Boaz, the kinsman-redeemer, points us to Jesus—our true Redeemer.

CHAPTER ONE

Renewing Our Direction

If you think unsavory political leaders, economic and environmental disasters, and prolonged wars are purely modern phenomena, then take a look at ancient Israel. In the first verse of the book of Ruth, we learn that the story took place during Israel's period of judges. According to Exodus 18:13–27, Moses appointed judges to serve as governors and protectors of the people of Israel. They were a mixed bag. The first judge was Othniel, one with a sanitized testimony—your typical churchman.

But the last judge was Samson, a roughneck who broke all his Nazirite vows. For example, he broke his vow to not to touch any dead thing when he scooped honey out of the carcass of a lion (Judges 14:9). Nor did he abstain from fermented drink, which was also a condition of the Nazarite vow (Judges 14:10).

To top it all off, he wanted to marry a Philistine woman (Judges 14:1)—an enemy of the Israelites! Clearly, some of the judges performed better as role models for the people than others did.

It was an era of Baal worship. Chapters 17 through 21 of Judges describe a cycle in which Israel seemed to repent of their idolatry for a season and then lapse back into it. The pull of the idols was so strong that the people eventually conformed to the surrounding culture, instead of transforming it.

So, God said, in effect, "Since you want to do things your way, and you only consult Me when you need something—I'll just step back."

Does this scenario sound familiar? God the Creator is still on the throne, although society at large ignores Him. Even His people, His redeemed ones, push the boundaries.

But God will have the last word, and one day His creation will be judged. Because He loves us, however, He gives us countless chances to turn to Him.

Salvation belongs to God, and His dealings with us have always reflected His amazing grace, with which He laces even His just judgments.

Despite our defiance, God has never abandoned His people. Throughout the millennia, His grace has never ceased for a moment. The story of Ruth is, above all, a story of grace.

Let's turn to the first two verses, which set the scene for our story:

> In the days when the judges ruled in Israel, a severe famine came upon the land. So a man from Bethlehem in Judah left his home and went to live in the country of Moab, taking his wife and two sons with him. The man's name was Elimelech, and his wife was Naomi. Their two sons were Mahlon and Kilion. They were Ephrathites

from Bethlehem in the land of Judah. And when they reached Moab, they settled there. — Ruth 1:1-2

From the choices Elimelech and Naomi made, we can derive basic insights into (1) where we should find direction in our decision-making, (2) how to make decisions, (3) why we must consider the consequences of our decisions, and (4) how our decisions interact with the purpose God has established for each of us.

Searching for Direction

Ruth 1:1 tells us that a famine had hit the land. Now, this calamity was more than a natural disaster. Judges 17:6 tells us there was no king and the people did "whatever seemed right in their own eyes." The famine recorded in Ruth chapter 1 was possibly part of God's judgment on the people, and Elimelech made the situation worse by deciding to relocate to Moab.

Elimelech's name meant "God is my King," but he hardly lived up to it. He had been living in Bethlehem (meaning "house of bread")—however, because of the famine, he moved his family to Moab, of all places.

Moab originated from an incestuous relationship between Lot and his daughter. As a result, Moab was excluded from "the assembly of the LORD"—that is, from the communal life of God's people—for "ten generations" (Deuteronomy 23:3). It was a morally corrupt place where Elimelech, as one of God's people, was not supposed to dwell. Thus, God had warned the Israelites not to "promote the welfare and prosperity of the Ammonites or Moabites" (Deuteronomy 23:6).

Yet Elimelech saw famine and fled Bethlehem to Moab. He allowed an attitude of faith to be overruled by a desire for comfort. God had delivered the people out of Egypt and brought Elimelech to Bethlehem, but the moment life grew difficult, he went to a morally corrupt country.

Sometimes we move to new places in search of greener pastures. We might be struggling in a particular season and think a change of scenery will be the key to our happiness.

However, it *could* be a case of plain disobedience. We can start to convince ourselves we are our own best counsel, but as Elimelech discovered, the greener pastures don't always deliver on their promises. In the end, we might find ourselves simply running away from God's plan for us.

Often something we expected to be delightful turns out to be disappointing. We travel in our own direction while God tells us, "Wrong way, wrong way!" And only when our decisions fail to bear good fruit, as the same bad things keep happening over and over, do we acknowledge He was right all along.

Perhaps God has said to us, "You've ignored the right way, and now you are aware of where your decisions have landed you. But I still love you, and you can turn back to Me at any time."

As we're sitting in that bleak place, however, it's hard to hear from God. We don't even want to read His Word, because we feel so embarrassed. And on the way to our dead end, we may have hurt others beside ourselves.

But there is still grace for us. If we are in that place now, we need to know how to respond.

Called to Uncomfortable Decisions

Are our decisions made as if there were no King in our life? If we claim to belong to Jesus, our choices should not be based merely on how we feel or on what seems right to us.

Yet that's how many of us make decisions today! We date because of how we think someone else will make us feel, and because it seems right to us. We relocate to different cities and we leave our church because it seems right to us to do so.

If our King is in charge, He will guide us when we make decisions: He can tell us what to do, where to go, and when. However, if we're honest, we really don't like this set-up—because at our core, many of us want to serve God on our own terms.

Don't assume our feelings of discomfort mean we're not in God's plan. In fact, the gospel is a call to discomfort!

Show me a comfortable prophet. Neither Isaiah nor Jeremiah lived a comfortable life. Paul endured many difficulties and wrote that we enter the Kingdom through much hardship (Acts 14:22).

Better yet, show me a comfortable Savior! Jesus left the richness of glory to come to earth.

But Jesus did not quit when the going got rough: "Father, if you are willing, please take this cup of suffering away from me. Yet I want your will to be done, not mine" (Luke 22:42) He was prepared to endure the unjust punishment awaiting Him.

This was in spite of the fact that Jesus understood what He was facing. By contrast, when Elimelech and Naomi moved to Moab, neither of them likely knew the long-term outcome:

> Then Elimelech died and Naomi was left with her two sons. The two sons married Moabite women. One married a woman named Orpah, and the other a woman named Ruth.
>
> But about ten years later, both Mahlon and Kilion also died. This left Naomi alone, without her two sons or her husband. Not only did Elimelech make a bad decision, but Naomi, Elimelech's widow, had made a bad decision by remaining in a corrupt place that had seemingly produced more misery than anything else for her family. — **Ruth 1:3–5**

Naomi, Ruth, and Orpah didn't know they would soon become widows. We don't always understand what is before us.

We're like the African impala, a beast that can jump ten feet in the air yet be enclosed within a three-foot wall in a zoo. Why? Because the impala will not jump if it can't see where its feet will land. Therefore, it chooses to remain in captivity.[1]

Many of us are the same way. Rather than trust God's plan and process, we stay in the three-foot enclosure of doing things our way. Rarely do we consider the consequences and collateral damage of making decisions this way. We think if we do things our way, we can predict or control the outcome—we presume to know where our feet will land.

However, like magic, control is an illusion.

Considering Consequences

Imagine you live in South Carolina and your spouse decides to take you and the family to North Dakota. You uproot your life and move out there. Then your spouse dies, leaving you stranded with two children.

That is the essence of what happened to Naomi. Naomi lost her husband in Moab, and soon she would lose her sons as well. She must have felt incredible loneliness!

Naomi now had the opportunity to go back to the land of her birth, the land to which God had led her. But what did she do? She decided to stay in Moab for ten more years!

Not only that, but her sons married Moabite women as well. Given the prohibition against intermarriage with various non-Jewish peoples in Deuteronomy 7:3, in combination with the restrictions against Moabites in Deuteronomy 23:2–4, we can reasonably suppose that marrying Moabite women was against God's wishes for His people.

To be clear, this had nothing to do with race, but with religion. God forbade religious intermarriage because He understands the importance of having a common view of eternity when it comes to relationships—which was the primary reason for His prohibition.

The family was from Bethlehem, so they knew God's commands as well as the biblical promises. They knew all about the miracles God did in the book of Exodus. Yet believing in or seeing miracles doesn't necessarily change us. The people of Israel saw God perform miracles firsthand but still worshiped a golden calf!

We are the ones who need to change, yet we naturally resist change that we can't control. We don't want anyone else interfering with our choices in our relationships or activities.

Then, when disaster strikes, many of us tend to blame God instead of ourselves. Indeed, in Ruth 1:13, Naomi described her circumstances as God raising His fist against her. But instead of questioning God, she should have questioned *herself*.

Isn't it funny the way we blame the Lord when we make decisions that ruin our life? *Somehow, God, it's your fault that I disobeyed You. Please fix it.*

Today, under normal circumstances, moving to a new place is no big deal—unless we're Christians. Our faith as believers has a bearing on where we live and whether we stay or go. Any move is significant if we call ourselves followers of Jesus, because all decisions have consequences.

If we don't have a renewed perspective when it comes to decision-making, we may find ourselves at a dead end despite our best efforts. Many of us have been there!

Naomi lost the most important men in her life, her husband and both of her sons, in an era when the men provided for the family. She must have wondered how she would survive.

God doesn't delight in our financial struggles, nor is He happy to see us unemployed. He doesn't take pleasure in the grief we face when we lose loved ones. He allows those things, however, because no loss needs to be wasted in His economy.

God didn't rejoice because Naomi lost her family. Rather, He rejoiced that her loss eventually led her back to Him.

You may be encountering immense difficulty right now. Perhaps you're experiencing a divorce, the loss of a child or loved one, bankruptcy, a short sale or foreclosure, depression, or a terminal illness. I want you to know that this difficulty isn't purposeless, nor is God trying to repay you for the sins of your past.

Remember, the beauty of the Christian faith is that death ends in a resurrection, meaning in Christ our darkest moments are only that: moments. They're not permanent, because our God defeated death (1 Corinthians 15:55–56).

The African church father Athanasius captured this reality beautifully in his book *On the Incarnation*:

> He, the Life of all, our Lord and Saviour, did not arrange the manner of his own death lest He should seem to be afraid of some other kind. No. He accepted and bore upon the cross a death inflicted by others, and those other His special enemies, a death which to them was supremely terrible and by no means to be faced; and He did this in order that, by destroying even this death, He might Himself be believed to be the Life, and the power of death be recognised as finally annulled. A marvellous

and mighty paradox has thus occurred, for the death which they thought to inflict on Him as dishonour and disgrace has become the glorious monument to death's defeat.[2]

You can't get any more permanent than death, which Christ defeated. Therefore, with Christ, victory is assured—it's a done deal.

Living in the Light

We see in 1 Kings 16–18 how God came down on the people because they were worshiping Baal. When God sees us worshiping false gods, He knows how to get our attention. Yet His judgment is always clothed in grace and is intended to bring about reconciliation.

Ruth lived in the period of judges when most people were Baal worshippers. They believed Baal owned the land and controlled its productiveness. Baal's female companion was a goddess named Ashtoreth, and when the two of them mated, it was believed it enhanced the productivity of the crops.

But God had commanded the people not to follow any false gods (Exodus 20:3–6) or associate themselves with the prosperity of certain idolatrous nations, including the Moabites (Deuteronomy 23:6). Why did He have to command this? Because sometimes when we are following God, it seems as if those who don't care about Him are better off than we are:

"Lord, I am trying to be holy and follow Your ways and I can't find a man, but *she* has five to choose from!

Lord, I've been filling out applications for a year now and this swindler easily gets work—you blessed *him* but not me?"

Let's be honest: we can feel like life is not fair sometimes. That's why we need *renewed direction.*

Israel had turned to idol worship because they undervalued their relationship with God and the community of His people. Because Israel failed to see the importance of living in the direction of obedience to God, including treating each other as a spiritual family, they lost their sense of trajectory. Instead, they grew accustomed to wallowing in spiritual darkness.

Have you ever been in a dimly lit restaurant? If so, you know that after a while, your eyes begin to adjust and you get used to the dark. Then, when you go back outside, the light hurts your eyes.

That's what happens to many of us. We get used to the dark as it relates to our lives and decision-making—a little compromise here and there, and the next thing we know, we are no longer convicted for things we shouldn't be doing. We stop monitoring what we allow into our lives, so over time we grow accustomed to the dark. Then nobody can tell if we're in God's kingdom or out of it, in terms of our lifestyle and decisions.

If we get used to the dark, the light can be most uncomfortable. The longer we stay in the dark, the more the light hurts. But thank God—the light is still there, waiting for us to return to the path and purposes He intends.

Moving into Our Purpose

Do we believe God can use us beyond our wildest dreams? We do not live where we live, or work where we work, simply because the job is there to pay our bills. We don't live in our home merely because we like the neighborhood or because it was all we could afford. We work where we work and live where we live because God wants us to change the atmosphere and the culture there for His glory. We are ambassadors for Christ if we are His disciples.

If we are thinking of moving in a particular direction, here are five purpose-driven questions we can ask ourselves to help us make the right decision:

"Why do I *want* to move?" "Why do I want to leave this church? Why do I want to date this person? Why do I want to change jobs? Am I being totally honest about my motives?"

Such questions empower us and propel us to be sober, mature decision-makers instead of being led by our emotions. Elimelech didn't do that, and the consequences were costly. Too often, we move or act on emotion and end up adding to the drama in our lives, rather than resolving it.

"What story do I want to tell?" Before we make any decision, we need to think about the testimony it will entail. How's it going to end? Will it be a story of disobedience or of obedience? Before you date this person, move to that city, or leave this ministry, think about the end.

We don't do this often enough. Instead, we live in the "now" so fully that we fail to realize our present will soon be our past—and will impact our future. Take a moment to think about the story that will arise from your decision, and have the self-awareness to pray about your decision-making process so you can break the cycle of bad decisions.

"Is there a tension associated with my choice?" If we are making a major decision and there is no tension, we should be concerned.

If we can easily pack up and leave a city, we probably have commitment issues. We probably don't stay anywhere or with anyone long-term. We may be church hoppers or people hoppers or job hoppers.

If there is no tension involved with our move, something could be wrong, because God doesn't plant us anywhere by accident.

"What would glorify God the most?" "Does it glorify Him more if I stay or if I leave?" This question is one of value. Too often, we want God to bless our plans rather than submitting to His. We rarely consider what will glorify God, because we're only thinking about our desires.

This is why Christ instructs us to seek His kingdom first (Matthew 6:33), because God knows we'll forget His kingdom while we're building ours.

Though this is easier said than done, we should value God's happiness above our own. Why?

Because God does everything for His glory and our good, glorifying Him may not seem or feel good in the moment. However, in the end, it will prove to be what's best for us.

"Do I have a sense of completion?" "Have I done what God wanted me to do here in this season?" As individuals, we may be fragile and finite, but God wants to use us to build His church on the gospel of Christ, for His sake. Can we say, before we leave this city, that we are spiritually ready to go?

If we ask ourselves these questions, the Lord will make His will plain to us.

Let's look at Ruth 1:3–5 again. Elimelech's decision to leave Bethlehem had severe consequences. Moab seemed like greener pasture, but it didn't produce what they really needed. When we make decisions with selfish motives, they never produce a true solution for our problems.

Apart from Christ and His purpose for our life, we'll never get that sense of satisfaction and completion we crave. We may try to take matters into our own hands, but we are not sovereign. It is impossible for us to know the outcome of our choices. In this case, Elimelech's decision to move in pursuit of food ended in his death.

Heeding God's Warning Signs

When we move in a particular direction, we sometimes end up in rough situations because we ignore the signs. I liken it to street signs, each with spiritual significance. God gives us a "Do Not Enter" and a "Wrong Way" sign before we end up at a "Dead End." Here is the breakdown:

Do Not Enter. This is a clear violation of Scripture. There's nothing to pray about because God has already declared what's right and what's wrong in His Word. Dating a non-believer (see 2 Corinthians 6:14), seeking revenge on someone who hurt you (see 1 Peter 3:9), and flirting with your attractive co-worker because your spouse is frustrating you or not making you happy (see Ephesians 5:25–32) would be examples of "Do Not Enter" signs in our lives. While the situation may be difficult, we're not justified in handling things our way as opposed to God's.

Wrong Way. This is when God speaks through obstacles and other people that this particular path is not His plan for us. However, God will speak through life and through others to guide you back to Him. The difficulty we're facing is self-inflicted affliction—a result of disobedience instead of obedience—but God is graciously allowing difficulty to arise to stop us from continuing down the path of destruction.

Dead End. This is when we're not bearing fruit. The decision isn't producing godly fruit, and it may be weighing negatively on our walk with God and our ability to hear Him. When we're at a dead end, we're trapped in a vicious cycle, and only confession and repentance (James 5:16) will lead us out.

If you're in such a place, don't think you're too far gone. Grace is available at any point to guide you back.

On the road to compromise, we've ignored a few "Wrong Way!" and "Do Not Enter" signs and coasted to a dead end. At the dead end, God tells us we will no longer produce fruit.

There is one road sign, however, that we won't see on the road to compromise: we'll never see a "No U-turn" sign. In His grace, God will always allow us to turn around. Our mess-ups never make us exempt from His grace.

So, we blew it—it's not the end of the world! We can respond by either blaming something or claiming something. *It's not our decisions that define us, but the way we respond to the* **consequences** *of our decisions.*

Take Naomi, for example. She could have said, "Elimelech led me out here to Moab, so it's his fault! … Okay, I stayed for ten more years, so I guess I can't keep blaming him. He died, and I chose to stay. But I'm still alive, and I can have a new direction!"

In the Old Testament, God's blessings and curses were often presented in physical circumstances. Today when someone disobeys God, we don't usually see them cut down on the spot. If we did, it might scare us, but it wouldn't change us for the long term. Lasting change requires a renewal of our hearts.

Therefore, for New Testament Christians, difficulties aren't always punitive—that is, they don't necessarily happen because of something we've done. Bad things happen simply because we live in a fallen world. But God can use our trying circumstances as part of the renewal process, and for His glory.

In other words, God sometimes puts us in a fix to fix *us*, which demonstrates grace on His part. With this in mind, we should stop trying to change our situation and realize *we* are what needs to change. In the words of Paul the Apostle:

> *Now I am glad I sent [the reproving letter], not because it hurt you but because the pain caused you to repent and change your ways. It was the kind of sorrow God wants his people to have, so you were not harmed by us in any way.* — **2 Corinthians 7:9**

Thus, we need not associate loss with defeat.

Moreover, if we have a renewed perspective and direction, it doesn't matter what happens because we know where we're going and how the story ends. We may not know what's around the corner, but as believers we've read the end of the Book and understand with whom the victory lies.

Right now, we may be struggling financially, our marriage may be rocky, and our kids may be defiant. We believe God will restore those situations, but even if He doesn't, we know the story ends with us worshiping Him in victory. If you're a believer reading this, you're not fighting *for* victory, but fighting *from* victory. Don't forget, if you're struggling with faith, there's grace for you and God wants you. It's not too late.

Making a U-turn

> *Then Naomi heard in Moab that the LORD had blessed his people in Judah by giving them good crops again. So Naomi and her daughters-in-law got ready to leave Moab to return to her homeland.* — **Ruth 1:6**

In many ways, this is an Old Testament version of the Prodigal Son story. Luke 15:11–32 records the story of a younger son who came to his dad requesting his share of the estate. At that time, the older son would typically get two-thirds of the father's estate and the younger son would get one-third. But it normally happened only after the father passed away. Thus, in effect, the younger son was saying he wished his father were dead.

Likewise, Elimelech's unfaithful actions in moving to Moab had implied, in effect, that he wanted God's provision without necessarily wanting God. This is how some of us operate. We want stuff from God, but we don't necessarily want *Him*.

In both Luke 15 and Ruth 1, there are similarities of disobedience, selfishness, greed, and loss—but there is also the similarity of God's amazing grace.

In the New Testament story, while the younger son was eating with the pigs—dealing with the consequences of his decision—he came to his senses and remembered he had a father back home. In Naomi's story, in the fields of Moab, she heard that God was again providing food in Bethlehem. In both cases, it was the father's love that drew them back home.

In the place of sin and disobedience, God speaks to us. We may have ignored the warnings and ended up in the land of compromise, but God will still allow us to come to our senses. He'll tell us we can still come home.

The prodigal son walked a long road back to his father's place. Likewise, Naomi walked a long road back to Bethlehem. Both returned to the arms of their Father.

Elimelech left a place of famine, seeking a blessing. Jesus left glory to *be* the blessing. Elimelech left Bethlehem, the House of Bread. Jesus is the Bread of life (John 6:35). Elimelech and Naomi left to build their own kingdom. Jesus brings the Kingdom of God to us (Luke 17:21). The grace of the Father is abundant in both of these stories.

Consider this question: Where did Naomi hear about the famine being lifted in Bethlehem? She heard about it in Moab, meaning in her place of disobedience. God ensured that she heard she could return home, and God does the same for you.

That's the essence of the gospel: we don't seek God, but He seeks us. He allows a divine U-turn by grace and through faith in Him.

If you're in such a place, it's not too late for you, because of His grace. Remember, *because of the grace God extends us, our failures aren't fatal.*

According to Ruth 1:6, Naomi made her U-turn and set off for Bethlehem. But even in turning back, she had low expectations. She did what she felt she had to do, without ever feeling she could be happy again. In the next chapter, we see her attitude beginning to change.

WORKBOOK

Chapter 1 Questions

Question: When in the past have your circumstances become so tough you wanted to give up on doing the right thing? What drove you to push forward in the light of God's Word and Spirit, despite the difficulty?

_____

_____

_____

_____

_____

_____

_____

_____

_____

_____

_____

_____

Question: What results have you experienced when you've tried to change your own situation, in your way, instead of listening to God's plan?

_____

_____

_____

_____

_____

_____

_____

_____

_____

_____

_____

Question: What kinds of signs did God use to reach you when you attempted to go in your own direction? What is an example of a "Wrong Way" sign that finally prompted you to make a U-turn in such a situation?

_____

_____

_____

_____

_____

_____

_____

_____

Action: Don't be disobedient to God by trying to solve your problems your way. Instead, run toward Him and persist in His light!

Chapter 1 Notes

CHAPTER TWO

Renewing Our Expectations

"There's no place like home!"
A simple yet profound biblical truth undergirds this time-worn phrase. Even when we are at our worst, God's judgment is always laced with grace. As we observed in the previous chapter, He continually extends the invitation for us to turn back and set things right.

Naomi should not have been in Moab, and she could not blame Elimelech for her situation because she had decided to remain there for ten years after his death. She had lost her husband and her two sons, and now she had only Orpah and Ruth by her side:

With her two daughters-in-law she [Naomi] set out from the place where she had been living, and they took the road that would lead them back to Judah.

But on the way, Naomi said to her two daughters-in-law, "Go back to your mothers' homes. And may the LORD reward you for your kindness to your husbands and to me. May the LORD bless you with the security of

*another marriage." Then she kissed them good-bye, and
they all broke down and wept.*

"No," they said. "We want to go with you to your people."

*But Naomi replied, "Why should you go on with me? Can I
still give birth to other sons who could grow up to be your
husbands? No, my daughters, return to your parents'
homes, for I am too old to marry again. And even if it
were possible, and I were to get married tonight and bear
sons, then what? Would you wait for them to grow up and
refuse to marry someone else? No, of course not, my
daughters! Things are far more bitter for me than for you,
because the LORD himself has raised his fist against me."*

*And again they wept together, and Orpah kissed her
mother-in-law good-bye. But Ruth clung tightly to Naomi.
"Look," Naomi said to her, "your sister-in-law has gone
back to her people and to her gods. You should do the
same." — Ruth 1:7–14*

Naomi was on her way home. Ruth 1:14 tells us her
daughters-in-law wept when she was about to separate
from them. Orpah kissed her mother-in-law goodbye, but
Ruth's stubborn loyalty earned her Naomi's rebuke.

"Your sister-in-law is going back to her people and
her gods," Naomi said. "Go back with her!"

You can almost hear the desperation and bitterness in
her voice. Sometimes when we experience loss or difficulty, we lose all hope. Imagining we are on our own, we
lower our expectations of God.

Expecting Too Little of God

The line of demarcation separating superficial faith
from substantive faith is *expectation*.

What if I were to tell you that without even knowing you, I know exactly what God is doing in your life right now? He's doing exactly what you expect Him to do. I'm not saying that you and I can control God. Nor am I implying that through positive thinking, you and I can somehow move God's hand. What I am saying is that many of you right now are experiencing exactly what you expect *because you don't expect God to do much through you.*

Matthew 9:29 records Jesus' healing of two blind men, during which Jesus says something vital: "Because of your faith, it will happen." The point is not believing God for whatever we want, but believing that He will be who He says He is—Creator, Healer, Redeemer, Messiah, Provider, Savior, and so on.

If we believe God to be God, then our expectations of Him should not fade over time, but rather increase. But why is this not the case for so many who claim to follow Jesus?

Decreased expectation (DE) is my term for an affliction that besets the life of many believers. Sometimes we harbor false assumptions about God and our relationship with Him—often because, in some way, we expect too little of Him or of other people. Over time, decreased expectation sets in.

Thankfully, there are identifying symptoms we can use to diagnose whether we ourselves might be suffering from DE:

1. We assume we know God's will without consulting Him.

Ruth 1:7 and Ruth 1:9, above, reveal something about Naomi's expectations. She had begun her journey back to Bethlehem and fully expected to go alone. Why? Perhaps because she had already lost her husband and two sons. Perhaps she just wanted to be alone. Or maybe she had made assumptions about the character of Orpah and Ruth.

Notice that Scripture says Naomi told them to go back to Moab, but it doesn't say she prayed about the matter. In other words, she assumed. Perhaps, too, she was expecting God to provide for her needs, without necessarily submitting to His will.

Remember, Naomi had left Bethlehem (the House of Bread) because of a famine and had migrated with her husband and sons to a land of moral corruption. Like many of us, Naomi enjoyed the illusion of control.

And it really is an illusion, because you and I are not sovereign. God is sovereign, however, and we should always check with Him before we make important decisions.

2. We believe we don't deserve to be loved.

Naomi tried to take control of her travel plans. Sometimes, because we feel we don't deserve God's love, we get so far away from Him that we act like we answer only to ourselves. This causes us to reject God's loving advances that come through other people as well.

Ruth 1:10 and 1:11 reveal Naomi's continuing assumption that she would be journeying back to the Promised Land alone. Orpah and Ruth both offered to accompany her, but Naomi asked, "Why *should* you go on with me?" She was assuming the only reason they would go with her would be to get new husbands. Think about that. Did she suppose they only wanted her company for what they could get from her? If so, it might have been because Naomi only wanted God for what *He* could do for her. Her error was in supposing everyone else shared the same selfish outlook.

We love conditionally, but we make a mistake if we think God loves that way. Sometimes we might wonder: "Why would You want to love me, God? Why would You want to be my Father when my earthly father has rejected me? Why would You promise to be with me when so many people have walked out of my life?

"How could I believe You would love me when I believe I'm beyond being loved? How could You forgive me when I've hurt so many people? How could anyone love me if they know all I've done?"

If we don't believe we can be loved, we have listened to a lie of the enemy. The gospel proves that you and I *are* lovable. Jesus died for us even though we had done nothing to earn it. We had nothing to offer Him—except our sin. That is the beauty of grace.

When we suffer from decreased expectations of God—because of disappointments, difficulties, or rejection—we reduce Him to the level of a human being whose love for us is based on our performance.

Naomi revealed the heart behind her rhetorical question, because she had already assumed her daughters-in-law wouldn't go with her. In fact, she didn't even *want* them to go with her! In Ruth 1:11 she asked, "Can I still give birth to other sons who could grow up to be your husbands?"

Naomi might have assumed she wasn't loved by Orpah and Ruth. Instead, she thought their only motive for accompanying her might be their own future prospects. Isn't it interesting how we can project our perspectives onto others? But even if that describes us today, we can still make a U-turn. We can renew our expectations of God.

Our decreased expectations can cause us to miss out on what God intends for us. We can be oblivious to the fact that He is showing us His love for us through others—or we may be misled into believing God is against us.

3. We believe God is against us.

When we experience disappointment, heartache, or betrayal—even if we are saved and have the Holy Spirit within us, and are aware God has forgiven our sins—we may start believing God is against us. Because when we suffer repeated rejection and disappointment, even if we have brought it on ourselves, it's easy to ascribe the blame to God.

In Ruth 1:12–13 we see Naomi's false belief that God isn't working in her favor. She says in verse 13, "The LORD himself has raised his fist against me."

How could she say that? *She* had decided to leave the House of Bread with her husband and to remain in Moab for ten more years after Elimelech died. For ten whole years, living in Moab had been her decision. Remember this: *pain is inevitable, but misery is a choice.* She chose to stay there ten more years, but God chose to show and shower her with love in the form of a message letting her know that the famine had been lifted—and a Moabite woman named Ruth who wouldn't take "no" for an answer.

You don't have to stay in your current place, either. If you do, you're choosing misery, which is not what God intends for you.

Naomi was overlooking the fact that it was not God who was against her—it was Moab, her place of disobedience and compromise. But God was working in her favor even though she was outside of His will.

Thus, in Ruth 1:6, while Naomi was in Moab, she heard that God had lifted the famine so she could return to Bethlehem. There was no way the hand of God was against Naomi! That was grace.

Jesus meets us in our place of disobedience and compromise, and He lets us know we can make a U-turn. We can turn to Him and receive His goodness, love, grace, acceptance, purity, and holiness.

We must not think God is against us when we face the negative consequences for our own actions. If we are Christ's disciples, all that God does and allows to occur works for His glory and our benefit—just as it did in Naomi's life.

4. We allow preconceived predictions to replace faith.

Naomi could believe God parted the Red Sea, and she could believe God sent ten plagues on Israel's enemies. Yet she found it hard to believe God could work in her life through a Moabite woman named Ruth.

This is clear in Ruth 1:14–15. Naomi was right about Orpah, but wrong about Ruth.

Orpah, whose name means 'neck,'[3] kissed her mother-in-law and showed her the back of her neck when she returned to Moab. Ruth, however, clung to Naomi. The Hebrew word for 'clung' is *davak*, and it carries a similar idea to the bond of marriage, in Genesis 2:24. It means this Gentile woman, who had nothing to do with Israel, was making a marriage-like commitment to a believer who had lost hope.

God was using a non-believer in the life of a believer. This showed the extent of His love.

Sometimes our expectations and assumptions are proven right, while other times God proves them wrong. Regardless, moments of apparent failure needn't dent our faith in who God is and what He can do through us or those around us. We must ask ourselves, *"Do I want to be right, or do I want Him to use me in the way He knows best?"*

Naomi was not experiencing the full potential of her faith. She and her husband apparently wanted God to meet their needs, and when God didn't seem to meet them in Israel, she sought prosperity in Moab. You and I often do the same thing. But God doesn't merely want to *meet* our needs—His intentions for us are far greater than that. He wants to *be* our greatest need.

We have within us the same Spirit that raised Christ from the dead, the same Spirit that empowered Christ to command hurricanes, the same Spirit that fell on Christ when He was baptized. That Spirit dwells in us, yet we remain focused on what we do or do not have. God wants to do so much more in and through us!

God works through us to meet lost people and bring them to Him. We don't always realize God is working in that way when He changes our circumstances or brings people to us. We are too busy thinking of our circumstances to be concerned for the lost.

5. We have a disregard for the lost.

Ruth said, "Don't urge me to leave you or to turn back from you. Where you go I will go, and where you stay I will stay. Your people will be my people and your God my God. Where you die I will die, and there I will be buried. May the LORD deal with me, be it ever so severely, if even death separates you and me." When Naomi realized that Ruth was determined to go with her, she stopped urging her. — *Ruth 1:16–18*

Naomi knew that Ruth, her Moabite daughter-in-law, was a non-believer. Notice in Ruth 1:15, she encouraged Ruth to go back to Moab, to her old religion. She was essentially saying, "Go back and worship your false gods."

When we are barely expecting God to meet our needs, we are not expecting Him to do mighty things in and through us. We begin to have a blatant disregard for the lost people around us.

A decreased expectation of God overtakes our life, and eventually we stop caring about others. We become inwardly focused and believe everything revolves around us. In Ruth 1:16–18, Naomi relented, but she didn't relent out of compassion. Rather, she relented out of frustration because of Ruth's persistence.

Isn't it interesting that Ruth, the non-believer, illustrated how intensely Christ loves us while Naomi, the believer, responded like a non-believer? Ruth encountered strong objections, yet she continued to say, "I am going to be with you. I am going to follow you. I am going to die with you." God used a non-believer who showed passionate commitment to demonstrate His kind of love!

6. We are bitter.

So the two women continued their journey. When they came to Bethlehem, the entire town was excited by their arrival. "Is it really Naomi?" the women asked.

"Don't call me Naomi," she responded. "Instead, call me Mara, for the Almighty has made life very bitter for me. I went away full, but the LORD has brought me home empty. Why call me Naomi when the LORD has caused me to suffer and the Almighty has sent such tragedy upon me?"

*So Naomi returned from Moab, accompanied by her daughter-in-law Ruth, the young Moabite woman. They arrived in Bethlehem in late spring, at the beginning of the barley harvest. — **Ruth 1:19–22***

When we stop caring about others and focus on our misery, we are bitter. Even though Naomi had gone home to her welcoming family and had something to which she could look forward, she was still bitter.

Naomi changed her name from Naomi, which meant "pleasant," to Mara, which meant "bitter." She resented God even though she had brought the distress on herself by disobeying Him. Yet God showed His grace by allowing her to make a U-turn back to Bethlehem, the House of Bread.

You may recall in Exodus 15:23–25, when God was leading the Israelites through the wilderness, they came to Mara and found the water was bitter. God told Moses to throw a log in the water and it became sweet. After Mara, they came to Elim, a place of rest.

When we go through Mara, there is always an Elim. Naomi did not have to stay in Mara, because Elim was coming.

Bitterness will do nothing but hurt us. Resentment only affects us and decreases our expectation of God. Bitterness about anything will affect our walk with God. But there is grace for us. We can turn back and expect God to do wonderful things in and through us.

Remember those times in the past when God provided? He provided jobs, checks in the mail, promotions, or a baby when doctors told us we couldn't have one. Even when tragedy hits and we lose the child or the marriage ends, He remains with us because that's what unconditional love is. It persists regardless of our response, and only God can love like this perfectly.

How could we doubt His love for us? We never have an excuse to throw in the towel!

Reasons Why People Give Up

There are three main reasons why people quit, and each begins with *T*.

First, life can simply be *tough*. It's easy to get angry with God and bail out when things get difficult. Frankly, life *is* tough—that's why we need a Savior—but so many Christians don't finish the race because it's just too hard. Jesus's disciples fell asleep on Him, but He still went to the cross.

Secondly, there is *tiredness*. Maybe we're tired of not getting results. But how are we defining 'results'? Is it just a matter of getting what we want?

True results are about producing godly fruit, because that's the only fruit that will last. Some of us are tempted to quit because it doesn't seem like God is coming through for us.

Have you ever felt like that? I have—but God reminds me, "I've given you all you need in Me!" That's why Paul encourages us:

So, my dear brothers and sisters, be strong and immoveable. Always working enthusiastically for the Lord, for you know that nothing you do for the Lord is ever useless.
— *1 Corinthians 15:58*

Thirdly, we may be *torn*. My brother Maliek has choreographed a beautiful dance to a song called "No Gray" by Jonathan McReynolds. The song talks about wanting to be saved yet really wanting to have one's cake and eat it, too. To be torn is to have a heart divided over something in this way—for instance, between God and money or between God and relationships. Ultimately, when we're torn, the problem is that we haven't given our heart over to God. Thus, we say: "God, I want You, but I need to see if this gig works out!" So, we put God on hold.

"Lord, I want You, but she's just too fine. She's a good person, but she's not feeling this church thing right now. I want to see how this goes with her. Let me check it out first."

"God, I want to represent You on campus, but they're having *fun*. Why would I want to turn that down? Here I am with my little 'God Is Not Dead' T-shirt, and I feel corny. If I'm honest, my heart is torn because I want their acceptance."

Was Jesus torn? In His humanity, He did say, "Father, if you are willing, please take this cup of suffering away from me" (Luke 22:42). But His devotion was always to God the Father, which is why He continued, "Yet I want your will to be done, not mine" (Luke 22:42).

Here is a word for us to pray daily:

Teach me your ways, O LORD, that I may live according to your truth. Grant me purity of heart, so that I may honor you. — Psalm 86:11

We need that prayer because like Naomi, we may often be tempted to give up.

Now the two women were arriving in Bethlehem. Ruth at this point had shown the love of Christ much more fully than Naomi had. Ruth had left Moab and everything familiar to her to make the journey to Bethlehem. Similarly, Christ left glory and came to earth to pay the price for our sin.

Naomi said she was empty, even though Ruth was with her. Christ emptied Himself for us, to identify with us and to redeem us (Philippians 2:7).

Ruth continued to pursue Naomi despite her continued rejection. Similarly, Christ pursued you and me to make us His children.

Naomi changed her name to "bitter" even while Ruth was with her. As Ruth persisted in loving Naomi, Jesus loves and pursues us through our prison of bitterness.

Expect God to Be Who He Says He Is!

Is your understanding of God a prison, as Naomi's was, or is it a safe haven?

Few things frustrate me more than hearing a Christian praying over someone for healing and concluding that prayer with the desultory disclaimer, "if it be Your will."

I have talked to countless suffering people who have said how discouraged they felt to hear those words. I am not saying we shouldn't pray for God's will, but if we are praying for healing, let's just *believe*.

God does not need you and me to remind Him of His sovereignty. God can heal who He wants in His own timing, but our place is simply to ask Him to do it.

Now, you may be wondering: How can I avoid being disappointed if God doesn't come through?" The answer is to fall back on Romans 8:28, which says, "God causes everything to work together for the good of those who love God and are called according to his purpose for them." We don't have to give way to disappointment, because we can trust God is working out everything—even the non-healing—for our benefit and for His glory.

We must believe God to heal, believe Him to deliver, believe Him to bring our rebellious child back, believe Him to save our marriage, believe Him to grow our church, believe Him to be God, and then trust Him with the outcome.

When we pray "if it be Your will," we may think we're showing suitable humility and surrender. Yes, we do want God's will to be done (Matthew 6:10). But sometimes we use the phrase as an escape clause because we don't really believe God is going to come through for us. It's a way for us to cover our bases.

"Jerome, are you suggesting that somehow our *expectations* can move God's hands?"

No, I am saying God wants us to plead, He wants us to believe, and He wants us to have these expectations. God sovereignly and lovingly responds when we pray and earnestly seek Him.

When King Hezekiah was seriously ill, he pleaded with God, and God responded to him by adding fifteen more years to his life (2 Kings 20). In the New Testament, the Lord said one kind of demon would "not go out except by *prayer and fasting*" (Matthew 17:21). We can pray to God fervently, earnestly, and unapologetically because He is our Father. He loves us and He wants us to live in expectation.

More Than We Ask or Imagine

Back in 2011, I had the choice to expect God to do something great or keep my safe predictions.

Vision Church was meeting in a converted theater complex. About six churches were using it simultaneously. The place we were in was okay, but we needed our own space and more freedom to do ministry. Therefore, in January I came before the church and said I was believing we would be in a new building on the first Sunday in August.

January rolled by. No building. February rolled by. No building. March rolled by. No building. Nor was there one in April, May, or June. I continued to pray and believe.

Then, in June, a funny thing happened. My assistant received an email from a guy named Troy Skora, who wrote: "I heard what you guys were doing in Washington Terrace and the Boys Club. We have this building and we're down to about eight people. We were wondering if you guys might be interested in using our building?"

I called that man immediately to tell him we were absolutely interested. We met with them and they came to hear me preach.

However, the process to finalize everything took a couple of months—and the first time they voted, the vote didn't go through. Soon it was July and crunch time, but I believed God was sovereign, and I continued to pray. In mid-July the vote passed, and the building was deeded over to us. We owned the church building, and we had our first service on the first Sunday in August—just the way I believed God would do it.

Now, I am not into the prosperity gospel because it's a false gospel that uses Christ as a means to an end. It represents "a different way that pretends to be the Good News but is not the Good News at all" (Galatians 1:6–7). Paul vehemently opposed and warned us to resist such twisted truths and their advocates (Galatians 1:8–9). God doesn't exist for our wants!

That said, it's okay to believe God is who He says he is. I believed God, and He blessed us with the building.

We still needed chairs a week before our first Sunday service in the new building. The building was old and only had pews. I got an email from one of our ministry partners asking, "How can I pray for you?"

I replied, "Chairs. We have this service coming up and we need chairs."

"Well, we are actually getting new chairs," he replied, "so we have a couple hundred chairs we can give you."

God came through with the building, God came through with the chairs, and we had our first service there. We praised, worshiped, and honored God for His faithfulness.

But there's more! The old building needed a lot of renovation. I was preparing something called the Vision Global Initiative. We were raising money to renovate our building, but also for our first mission trip to Cambodia. As I was typing a letter to send out to the church, I got a text from one of our ministry partners, Kevin Peck. He said, "Do you guys need $6,000?"

At first, I was trying to wrap my mind around the text. I took a screenshot and called the writer at once.

"Absolutely, we could use $6,000," I told him. We are trying to renovate our building."

As I was talking to him, he said, "You know what? I'm going to see if I can approve another $5,000. I'm pretty certain I can get that approved."

The $6,000 went up to $11,000! I hung up and called one of the elders at Vision Church, where I pastor.

"Pastor Irvin, you are never going to believe what's happened," I said. As I was talking to him, Kevin beeped in again. "Not only are we going to give you $11,000," he said. "I talked to a buddy of mine, who talked to his elders, and they cleared another $10,000!"

(Clearly, suburban ministry issues—"$10,000 laying around." I've never had that problem.)

So, a few minutes after being promised the chairs, we also received a text message and a phone call promising a total of $21,000. I hadn't even finished typing the fundraising letter. After that, we raised $9,000 internally. God thus came through with $30,000 to renovate the building He had given us for free, and He gave us chairs to sit on.

As Paul wrote to the Ephesians, "Now all glory to God, who is able, through his mighty power at work within us, to accomplish infinitely more than we might ask or think" (Ephesians 3:20).

Living in Expectation

Do we live with that type of expectation? Are we believing God for things while also rejoicing that He can do more than we ask or imagine?

You may be a ministry leader for whom things aren't going the way you had hoped. Is it looking as if God might not come through?

Listen, God will provide for His church because it's *His* church. He'll also take care of his children—even the disobedient ones like Naomi, like me, and like you.

Are you living in reduced expectation? Perhaps you're a mom who is doubting you can do much for God until your children are grown. That's a lie!

Perhaps you're thinking you can't start a ministry until you get everything in place. That's a lie, too! At some point, you must simply trust God and step out in faith.

I'm not saying we shouldn't plan. Our involvement and effort are required, but if we had everything we needed right now, we wouldn't need faith. We must expect God to be God.

We must not allow a weak expectation of God to undermine our life and our faith.

First, let us ask for an attitude of thanksgiving and pray with it daily. If we start our prayers by thanking

God, we will discover we have more for which to be thankful than we do about which to be bitter.

Secondly, let us expect God to do great things in us, through us, and around us. God doesn't want to merely meet our needs—He wants to use us in the city where we live. He wants us to impact the world for His glory.

Thirdly, let us ask the Holy Spirit to cultivate a spirit of expectation in us. If we start the day expecting to be used by God, we will be.

While Naomi was in disobedience, she focused on herself, yet God still showed her grace and compassion. Imagine how things could have been if she had demonstrated an attitude of thanksgiving, expecting God to do great things!

In Naomi's bitterness, she only expected her misery to continue, but God wanted so much more for her. Naomi needed to renew her expectation. A popular song goes, "Lord, what a difference a day makes!"[4] Better still, what a difference a new perspective makes.

We have seen the importance of renewing our expectation. Now, in the next chapter, we will address renewing our perspective.

WORKBOOK

Chapter 2 Questions

Question: Which of the false assumptions about God addressed in this chapter pose challenges to you in your daily life? How can you remind yourself that each of these assumptions is false?

_____

_____

_____

_____

_____

_____

_____

_____

_____

_____

_____

_____

Question: What is an experience you have had in which you wanted to give up, but persevered anyway? What led you to keep going? How has God encouraged you to press on through difficult circumstances?

_____

_____

_____

_____

_____

_____

_____

_____

_____

_____

_____

Question: What are your specific expectations for God? To what extent has He fulfilled or exceeded those expectations? How has He changed your expectations of Him?

_____

_____

_____

_____

_____

_____

_____

_____

_____

_____

_____

Action: Begin every day and every prayer by thanking God. Don't underestimate Him or His love for you, but expect Him to accomplish great things in your life, for you and through you—beyond anything you've imagined!

Chapter 2 Notes

_____

_____

_____

_____

_____

_____

_____

_____

_____

_____

_____

_____

_____

_____

_____

_____

_____

_____

_____

_____

_____

_____

_____

_____

_____

_____

_____

CHAPTER THREE

Renewing Our Perspectives

In Western political and family life, perhaps especially in American society, people tend to be obsessed with two core values: *freedom* and security, or *control*. The problem is that both of these values are illusions. We know *freedom* is an illusion when we stop paying our mortgage, or when we exceed the speed limit. We know control is an illusion when something totally unexpected happens and derails our plans.

The truth is, there are structures in place that ensure we don't get to do whatever we want. We might have thought freedom was having complete freedom of choice. We might have assumed we are free because we had the right to do what we wanted when we hit a certain age.

If we're honest, however, we will acknowledge that some of those "freedoms" led us into toxic situations, if not bondage. Perhaps we thought a certain job, person, or city would bring us real freedom, but in reality, we needed a renewed perspective on life.

The second illusion is *control*. We think we are in control until we find out there are things we can't control—such as our parents, where we were born, and our race. We all have a degree of control, but usually we're not sure quite how much we have.

If you are an unbeliever, atheist, or anti-theist, this probably frustrates you because it flies in the face of a culture that declares we can define and express ourselves however we choose—however we feel or desire—without regard to God or His Word.

In fact, in today's culture, people redefine God to justify their opinions and their self-selected identities. Yet the longer you live, the more you will realize the limitations of your control of your life and the world around you. And ultimately, declaring your freedom from God works to your own detriment, not your well-being or your happiness.

Living Within God's Boundaries

Although it's an illusion, we still fight for the right to do what we want, when we want, and how we want. But if we are truly in Christ, we understand freedom differently. We define it as *living within the boundaries set by God* (see Psalm 16:6).

As the gospel transforms us and renews our direction, we no longer make decisions based only on what makes us feel good. When we give our life to Christ, we give all our rights over to Him. It's not that we ask God to bless our will—rather, we submit to *His*.

Frankly, no one does this perfectly. None of us, not even the pastor, submits every decision perfectly to God! But we do need to pursue aggressively the perspective that our life is not our own.

I am a living sacrifice because Christ sacrificed Himself for me. And because of that, I live with the realization that I am not in control of my own life. The Bible says that "wherever the Spirit of the Lord is, there is [true] freedom" (2 Corinthians 3:17). But in God, the boundary "lines have fallen for me in pleasant places"! (Psalm 16:6 ESV) The restrictions God places on us are for our protection.

My son wakes up early in the morning. All of our rooms are upstairs, so we have a gate at his door. We don't want him to wake up at one in the morning and fall down sixteen stairs. The gate is there to protect him, not to restrict him unnecessarily.

God likewise protects us with limitations and restrictions, which is how we need to view the boundaries in our lives. When He sets limits, God is saying there are some places we're not to go, because He loves us. There are some things in which we are not to put our hope, because He loves us.

We need to trust that these boundaries are for our good. Do we live with that perspective every day?

Some prefer to think experience is the best teacher, but it's actually the *worst* teacher because it gives us the exam without the preparation! So instead of living by experience, we need to live by the truth of God's Word—which is not a collection of sixty-six unconnected fables. It's one story, told through sixty-six books, of a real God coming to redeem His wayward children.

Relinquishing the illusion of control is the path to freedom that counts. If we think freedom is being able to do whatever we want, it will lead us to a dead end. We need the perspective that freedom—true freedom—is living within the boundaries Christ has set for us.

Dead-End Perspectives

Without Christ, man determines what spiritual freedoms he chooses. These freedoms only lead to a dead end. Let's now look at several examples of dead-end perspectives.

As an essential element of Hinduism, *karma* is not something in which believers should put their faith. Yet we frequently hear people talking about "bad karma"! Karma is the idea that bad things happen to bad people and good things happen to good people.

The problem with that is, who defines what is good? Do you get to be your own guide? We could look at Jesus, a man who was betrayed, hungry, homeless, thirsty, and wrongly crucified—yet He was perfect! It's not true that bad things only happen to bad people and only good things happen to good people. If that were the case, Jesus wouldn't have suffered as He did.

A second dead-end perspective is *positivity*, the religion of the hip-hop generation. Though I'm a fan of hip-hop as a music genre, we must reject some of the philosophical perspectives championed by many of its representatives.

Essentially, positivity is the idea that if you simply put enough positive energy into the atmosphere, it's going to boomerang back on you. Accordingly, you make positive confessions and place faith in your confession, not necessarily in a higher power. This means you need to speak things out in order to create a new reality. By contrast, the Bible presents the reality that the only one who can speak things into existence is the God who spoke the earth into existence (Romans 4:17).

Positivity is also *subjective*. The object of someone's positive attitude might be morally empty or false. I can be positive but still treat women as objects and applaud men with "sidepieces" (women they see for sexual pleasure while being involved with someone else). Thus, positivity doesn't always carry any moral weight.

It's well and good to be positive, but a positive perspective has no saving value. Cultural relevance does not prove eternal significance. Rather, what truly matters is conformity to the moral and spiritual code God has laid out for us in His Word.

A third dead-end perspective is *spiritual syncretism*, the idea that all roads lead to the same place. However, this idea doesn't hold up long to scrutiny. If all roads have different destinations, how can they possibly lead to the same place?

The Muslim must earn his way to his place of eternity, while the Buddhist is trying to reach a place called nirvana, which is eternal nothingness. On the other hand, the Christian believes that Jesus Christ is the only way to eternal life with God. The Christian knows eternity is granted by grace and through faith, not earned. How then, can all roads lead to the same place?

And if my truth says your truth is a lie, is it still truth? We need to use the brains God gave us, and the Bible is clear that there is only one way—the Way of Jesus.

Man might choose these dead-end perspectives, but God remains faithful to all mankind. He loves us and intervenes for us, even when we don't realize His providence for us.

God in His Providence

Providence is a beautiful word that sums up all of God's activity in the world, including how He provides for humanity, especially for those who love Him.

One commentary says God's providence is a manifestation of God caring about the universe and everyone in it.[5] Throughout the centuries of human existence, many people have taken great comfort in God's providence. They have trusted God to go before them and prepare the way through the difficult places of life.

Providence is the evidence that God has not left this planet alone in the vast universe or forgotten the human situation for a moment. God visits, touches, communicates, controls, and intervenes. He comes before and between people and their needs. Providence is the reason we can be thankful in all seasons.

In other words, there are no accidents—and that includes us! God's providence applies regardless of the trials we face. God is orchestrating things in our life because He loves us.

No one was born saved. But in the providence of God, as the director of history, He has worked things out to bring us back to Him.

This is the renewed perspective we need. It's not complicated. In fact, it's truly simple! God's providence provides comfort for all of life's circumstances because it is the *reality*. We'll have some rough days, we'll lose some people, and we'll lose some things. And if our hope is in these temporal people or things, we'll experience immense pain.

But God is *providential*. In other words, He is in control. Moreover, He's working everything out for His glory, first and foremost, but also for *our good*.

There is a caveat, however: we must submit to Him. Our submission doesn't control His providence, because He is in control no matter what. But if we don't submit, we face judgment. That's what you and I faced, but God's grace and His providence worked things out to bring us back to Him:

> By his divine power, God has given us everything we need for living a godly life. We have received all of this by coming to know him, the one who called us to himself by means of his marvelous glory and excellence. — *2 Peter 1:3*

In effect, God is giving us all things, including a renewed perspective on *life*.

This is why we need a renewed perspective. Sometimes we complain so much about what we've lost that we miss what God is bringing to us at exactly the right time. This is where Naomi found herself.

Naomi and Ruth Experience Providence

Let's look at Ruth chapter 2 to understand God's providence a bit better:

> There was a wealthy and influential man in Bethlehem named Boaz, who was a relative of Naomi's husband, Elimelech.
>
> One day Ruth the Moabite said to Naomi, "Let me go out into the harvest fields to pick up the stalks of grain left behind by anyone who is kind enough to let me do it."
>
> Naomi replied, "All right, my daughter, go ahead." So Ruth went out to gather grain behind the harvesters. And as it happened, she found herself working in a field that belonged to Boaz, the relative of her father-in-law, Elimelech.
>
> While she was there, Boaz arrived from Bethlehem and greeted the harvesters. "The LORD be with you!" he said.
>
> "The LORD bless you!" the harvesters replied.
>
> Then Boaz asked his foreman, "Who is that young woman over there? Who does she belong to?"
>
> And the foreman replied, "She is the young woman from Moab who came back with Naomi. She asked me this morning if she could gather grain behind the harvesters. She has been hard at work ever since, except for a few minutes' rest in the shelter." — **Ruth 2:1–7**

To understand the full significance of this passage, we must look back at Ruth 1:22:

> So Naomi returned from Moab, accompanied by her daughter-in-law Ruth, the young Moabite woman. They arrived in Bethlehem in late spring, at the beginning of the barely harvest.

At the end of that first chapter, we learned that Naomi and Ruth arrived during the barley harvest. Here we begin to see how God's providence renews our perspective on life.

Naomi had lost her husband, Elimelech, and both of her sons. Moreover, her only companion was a Moabite woman—tantamount to a Gentile. However, this poor and hungry woman had, in God's providence, arrived just when the food was ready!

Naomi and Ruth's arrival at harvest time was both crucial and providential. The fact that they returned precisely when the food was ready was not "luck," because there is no such thing as luck. We have a God who is involved, and for whom there is no coincidence.

Now Naomi was back in Bethlehem. She was still childless, still with a social outcast, and still bitter. But God was at work.

In Ruth 2:4–7, the narrator wants us to see that God's providence is at work in His perfect timing. In view is the Hebrew word *checed* (or *hesed*). This is a rich theological term that encapsulates God's faithfulness and mercy.[6]

Here God's *checed* resulted in Him working things out for Naomi's good, even though she didn't appreciate it because of her bitterness. This is the God we serve!

God was showing Naomi that He was in control and aware of her needs. Remember how, at the end of Ruth chapter 1, she had asked others to call her Mara (meaning "bitter") instead of Naomi (meaning "pleasant"). She had chosen to be bitter about life, but God was still blessing her.

Yes, she had let Him down ten years earlier by remaining in Moab. And now, not only was He letting her come back to Bethlehem, but He was letting her come back at the right time so He could feed and clothe her as well. That's His goodness.

Have you ever been devastated by a breakup? If you've ever wept or not eaten, you know a bit about Naomi's grief. Having lost her husband and her two sons, she now felt she had nothing left.

We all hurt when we lose a spouse or a child, but the hard reality is, the people in our lives are temporary. Even *we* are temporary. This flesh of ours isn't going to last forever! Our skin will wrinkle, our knees will begin to crack when we walk, and some of us will experience pain simply by waking up.

That's not morbid—it's the truth. We can Botox ourselves all we want, but under the Botox are the wrinkles God preordained.

Wrinkles are a part of life, and placing our hope in temporary things and temporary people will only let us down.

When Naomi lost her husband and sons, her frustration caused her paralysis of faith. Now that she was older, she didn't even think about going out to find a new husband. Ruth, however, did hold such hopes.

How Does the Gospel Renew Our Perspectives?

Naomi was a bitter old woman who thought she had nothing to which she could look forward in her remaining years. She was traveling with a woman for whom she had held scant regard. Her past mistakes consumed her mind, and she had given up on God.

But God hadn't given up on her.

The Bible has answers for all of these concerns Naomi harbored. In what ways does the gospel renew our perspectives?

The gospel renews our perspective on *time*.

Naomi may have allowed her perception of time to cloud her judgment. Ten years is a long time to stay in the wrong place, but Ruth chapter 2 recounts the transformation that can happen in *one day!*

In one day God undid ten years of history, because He is not restricted by time. We waste time, but we serve a God who redeems it.

Naomi arrived at exactly the right moment. However, because she was still bitter, she didn't make the most of her time and missed some opportunities.

The gospel renews our perspective on *opportunities*.

Some of us have lost things. Maybe we've lost a job, whether recently or a year ago. Perhaps we've been hopping from job to job, or are simply frustrated in our current job: "I have a degree and am overqualified for this work. I shouldn't be in this position!" With such an attitude, we miss out on the other opportunities God provides.

Naomi was hungry and had the opportunity to go and get some food. Instead, she told her daughter-in-law, "Go ahead, Ruth!" Because Naomi was still wrestling with bitterness, she was experiencing a kind of paralysis. While not physically incapacitated, we can lose our godly ambition and stop dreaming.

Let's never stop dreaming! Let's never imagine God is done with us. If there is breath in our bodies, there are things God wants to do through us. And we can either regret the opportunities we've missed or focus on the opportunities before us.

Returning to Bethlehem and working hard was an opportunity. God used Ruth's forward-looking ambition to give hope to Naomi and allow her to dream again.

First, Naomi and Ruth essentially had to join Bethlehem's welfare program.[7] That's how poor people survived back in Naomi's day. In the fields after the workers had harvested the crops, the farmers would allow the poor to come and get the leftovers. But they had to work to get it themselves.

As a result, there was some dignity in this form of welfare. It was a kind of step-up ministry that enabled those with needs to provide for their families. Indeed, this was the first step of a new opportunity for Naomi and Ruth.

The gospel renews our perspective on *people*.

Naomi didn't want Ruth to come with her back to Bethlehem because Ruth was socially unacceptable. She was a non-Israelite woman from Moab. But God always calls those who don't belong, so Naomi had to recalibrate her perspective.

Ruth was going out to get food for this woman who had told her, "Don't you come back with me!" Naomi had rejected Ruth, but Ruth was showing her the love of Christ. God was using this non-Israelite woman in the life of Naomi to show her how those in the "chosen race" should behave. That's how God frequently operates.

Remember, Ruth said, "Your people will be my people, and your God will be my God" (Ruth 1:16). She turned her back on false gods and was turning toward the truth. God was truly at work!

Boaz went over and said to Ruth, "Listen, my daughter. Stay right here with us when you gather grain; don't go to any other fields. Stay right behind the young women working in my field. See which part of the field they are harvesting, and then follow them. I have warned the young men not to treat you roughly. And when you are thirsty, help yourself to the water they have drawn from the well."

Ruth fell at his feet and thanked him warmly. "What have I done to deserve such kindness?" she asked. "I am only a foreigner."

"Yes, I know," Boaz replied. "But I also know about every-thing you have done for your mother-in-law since the death of your husband. I have heard how you left your fa-ther and mother and your own land to live here among complete strangers. May the LORD, the God of Israel, un-der whose wings you have come to take refuge, reward you fully for what you have done."

*"I hope I continue to please you, sir," she replied. "You have comforted me by speaking so kindly to me, even though I am not one of your workers." — **Ruth 2:8-13***

In verse 8, Boaz, the kinsman-redeemer, called Ruth his daughter. His words to her were the first kind ones recorded in the book of Ruth. In this, Boaz was pointing us to the way Jesus treated the outsider. That's why she was blown away: "What have I done to deserve such kindness?" God, too, deals with us out of His grace.

No matter how severely we have sinned against Him, He calls us His child when we come home.

Could we be missing God's Word to us because we don't like the packaging of a person He sends to us? We don't like their race, we don't like how they dress, and we don't like the way they talk, but God may want to use that "outsider" in our life.

Boaz shows us how Jesus treats us. He doesn't look at our sin and then withdraw from us. Rather, He looks at our sin and says, "I want to take that! Come to Me rec-ognizing you are a sinner in need of a Savior. I don't need your so-called righteousness or feel-good positivity. Simply give Me your sin, and I will give you My Spirit. Come to My table!"

The gospel renews our perspective on our *experiences.*

Ruth was an outsider, but she was becoming a believer. She was seeking faith in the God of Israel, the one and only true God. Her decision to leave Moab was an act of faith, showing dedication not only to her mother-in-law but also to the Lord. In Ruth 1:19, Ruth wasn't even acknowledged. The relatives greeted Naomi as if Ruth weren't even there. The Moabite women were notorious for sleeping with the men of Israel to influence them to worship false gods.

Of course, this doesn't excuse the actions of the men, because it takes two to tango. However, in a culture rife with misogyny, Moabite women were especially ostracized by the people of Israel. Therefore, the Israelite women had a preconceived notion about Ruth without actually knowing her.

Notice how Ruth dealt with her experience as an outsider. She might have felt like nobody wanted her in Bethlehem because she was a Gentile. But she demonstrated faith, which God used—and Boaz heard about it.

We don't know who is watching us and what God is doing through us. We don't know the effect of the decisions we make.

If you are a Christian, what do people see when they look at how you live?

Remember, we do not work where we work just to pay the bills. Rather, God has a purpose for us in our workplace. We work where we work and live where we live to be a witness for Christ. We have families so we can be missionaries—as examples of godly living to each other, to those of other faiths, and to those without faith.

Do our romantic relationships reflect that we know Him? Does our conduct at work reflect that we know Him? Does everything we do reflect that we know Him? Our faith in God is going to draw attention, but we should always point people back to the Lord.

Moreover, when Boaz noticed Ruth, a love story was beginning to unfold. It was a demonstration of the redemption process—a picture of what Christ would do for the entire world.

> At mealtime Boaz called to her, "Come over here, and help yourself to some food. You can dip your bread in the sour wine." So she sat with his harvesters, and Boaz gave her some roasted grain to eat. She ate all she wanted and still had some left over.
>
> When Ruth went back to work again, Boaz ordered his young men, "Let her gather grain right among the sheaves without stopping her. And pull out some heads of barley from the bundles and drop them on purpose for her. Let her pick them up, and don't give her a hard time!"
> — Ruth 2:14–16

Ruth had come to Boaz empty-handed, just as we come empty-handed to the Lord. Let's stop thinking we need to bring a degree of righteousness to God. Remember, Boaz was *not* Jesus, but he does point us to Jesus. He was a kinsman-redeemer, but Jesus is the Redeemer of all humanity.

The gospel renews our perspective on *the lost.*

By all accounts, Ruth appeared to have come to faith. She said, "Your God will be my God." But notice how Boaz treated her even though she was still technically an outsider. His is an attitude we as Christians need to understand and emulate.

We want people to join our family, but they're not going to come to us air-brushed to perfection. Like Ruth, they're not going to come saying the right things, wearing the right clothes, or using the right language. They're going to come empty-handed, just as we once did.

The only thing we could offer Jesus was our sin. Sometimes our churches seem to cater specifically to our members, but others will come, and they may not be up to our standards. Some may appear to be more polished, but under every flower is *dirt*. And all of us have some of that.

This renewed perspective on the lost is part of God's providence. He is orchestrating things, so we shouldn't view a lost person as a lost cause. According to Acts 15:19, James said his "judgment is that we should not make it difficult for the Gentiles who are turning to God." In other words, we should not make it hard for people to come into our faith community.

Boaz called Ruth "daughter" and welcomed her to sit at his table. Once she got there, he supplied her with food and invited her to come back anytime.

That's what we are called to do. We are to invite people into our community, invest in them through discipleship, and inspire them to do the same thing in turn.

So Ruth gathered barley there all day, and when she beat out the grain that evening, it filled an entire basket. She carried it back into town and showed it to her mother-in-law. Ruth also gave her the roasted grain that was left over from her meal.

"Where did you gather all this grain today?" Naomi asked. "Where did you work? May the LORD bless the one who helped you!" — **Ruth 2:17–19**

At this point, Naomi didn't know it was Boaz, the man to whom she was related. She didn't know God was still working, but she was grateful for the food. Therefore, Ruth told her mother-in-law about the man in whose field she had worked. She said, "The man I worked with today is named Boaz."

Boaz, as the redeemer, had the role of inviting, investing in, and loving the lost. He was pointing us to Jesus.

God was using Ruth to inspire Naomi to trust in Him again. And when she saw all the food, she finally turned the corner!

Remember, she thought God was not on her side. She had said, in Ruth 1:13, that the Lord had raised His fist against her. This wasn't true, but sometimes we are tempted to feel the same way when we encounter rough times.

However, God continues to work in spite of our doubt, using our difficulties to prune us and make us more like Him. We should trust that He loves us, even when we experience hardships.

"May the LORD bless him!" Naomi told her daughter-in-law. "He is showing his kindness to us as well as to your dead husband. That man is one of our closest relatives, one of our family redeemers."

Then Ruth said, "What's more, Boaz even told me to come back and stay with his harvesters until the entire harvest is completed."

"Good!" Naomi exclaimed. "Do as he said, my daughter. Stay with his young women right through the whole harvest. You might be harassed in other fields, but you'll be safe with him."

So Ruth worked alongside the women in Boaz's fields and gathered grain with them until the end of the barley harvest. Then she continued working with them through the wheat harvest in early summer. And all the while she lived with her mother-in-law. — **Ruth 2:20–23**

What exactly was a kinsman-redeemer? Leviticus 24:25–55 tells us that a kinsman-redeemer was responsible for his extended family. For example, if a man's brother died, he took responsibility to care for the widow and her children. In some cases, if they were in debt and sold themselves into slavery, he would "redeem" them or buy them back.

This kinsman, Boaz, was related to Naomi's husband, Elimelech, who had died, which made him their kinsman-redeemer.

Naomi didn't even know that God was working behind the scenes through someone in her husband's family. Boaz's faith in God enabled him to stay in Bethlehem during the famine, and his abundance was now overflowing into the life of someone who had left. God thus uses faithful people in our life to bless us. Ultimately, we don't put our hope in people, but God may use others to bring us into a place of abundance. Ruth left their house that day empty-handed, but she came back full after she met the redeemer. Similarly, we come to God empty-handed, but we leave filled when we encounter our Redeemer.

The gospel renews our perspective on *God*.

It's not enough to renew our perspective on time, opportunities, people, experiences, and the lost. We must also renew our perspectives on our view of God.

How do we view God today? Is He waiting for us to mess up so He can punish us? Perhaps we don't say as much, but some of us live that way. We may love others conditionally, but God doesn't.

We think God is waiting for us to blow it again so He can come down hard on us. Naomi went through life thinking like this for many years. But that's not how He works! God was giving Naomi a divine do-over, something He has done in your life and mine.

Look at God's faithfulness. Elimelech's family had left Bethlehem to go to Moab, but Boaz had stayed. Many of Jesus' friends left Him (John 6:66), too, but our Redeemer stayed on the cross.

God was saying to Naomi, "Your husband made a bad decision, but there is still someone in your family whom

I am going to use, to give you another chance." Thus, God gave Naomi another chance, which led her to a new perspective—a *renewed* perspective.

Do we thank God for our divine do-overs? How many of them have we needed? Can we even count them? How many times have we messed up, yet God has given us another chance? These experiences should transform our perspective on God.

God is working to accomplish something in our lives. Think about the godly legacies we could leave if we took Him at His Word!

Maybe we didn't come from a Christian home—I didn't. But God and His providence are still at work. He is the One who saves the outsider—including each of us, who used to be outsiders like Ruth. We are the Moabites whom He called back and brought into His family.

Therefore, let's meditate on His goodness in our lives and cultivate both an attitude of thanksgiving and an eternal perspective. When we renew our perspectives, it is much easier to live within God's boundaries and see His providence.

Now, in the next chapter, we'll encounter a human love story—and a divine one, too.

WORKBOOK

Chapter 3 Questions

Question: When has your desire for freedom or control led you into a dead-end experience? How did God try to reach you in that situation?

_____

_____

_____

_____

_____

_____

_____

_____

_____

_____

_____

Question: What are some specific boundaries God sets for us? How do these boundaries provide you with real freedom? How is the boundary of time a form of God's providence?

_____

_____

_____

_____

_____

_____

_____

_____

_____

_____

_____

Question: How has God in His grace met a pressing need you had, or provided a path forward where none seemed to exist? How did His providence defy your expectations and reframe your perspective on a person, an opportunity, or God Himself?

_____

_____

_____

_____

_____

_____

_____

_____

_____

_____

_____

Action: Thank God for the limits He sets on us! Live within the boundaries He sets, and let Him transform your perspectives as you experience the genuine freedom of living by His providence.

Chapter 3 Notes

_____

_____

_____

_____

_____

_____

_____

_____

_____

_____

_____

_____

_____

_____

_____

_____

_____

_____

_____

_____

_____

_____

CHAPTER FOUR

A Renewal of Love

"It was true love."

"We're in love."

"I will always love you, no matter what."

Such phrases may be commonplace, but we rarely reflect on the full weight of their meaning—especially, on that four-letter word, 'love.'

Musiq Soulchild addresses the fickle nature of how people love in his appropriately titled song *Love*. The chorus is a powerful picture of love's ups and downs, but its final line captures the key to an attitude of faithful love: "For better or worse I still will choose you first."[8]

When you hear the word 'love,' what's the first thing that comes to mind? Perhaps you remember your first love, or maybe you think about your spouse and recall standing at the altar, saying "I do."

Or perhaps for you, it's more of a parental feeling. You think about the love you have for your child or your children.

And hopefully you think about the love God has for you.

It's such a beautiful thing to be loved and to have the privilege of loving someone in return. Yet love is also a complex subject, worth examining from different angles because doing so raises some difficult questions:

- Should a woman initiate love? (That's definitely something we see in this text.)
- Can we fall *out* of love?
- Can we love two or more people?
- And what *is* love, anyway?

The way love is portrayed in our American culture—what it is and how it works—opposes what God's Word says about it. Our culture idolizes physical appearance and makes sex the primary expression of love. (Listen to any R&B or pop song if you don't believe me!)

And sadly, many people who claim to know Christ have embraced the idea that love is all about how a person looks and how they perform in bed.

Because we understand love that way, we talk of people falling *out* of love. Then marriages collapse, and God's church is mocked because supposedly there is just as much divorce within it as there is in the world.

Yet we claim to know the deep truth of unconditional love! Therefore, we need a renewed perspective on the subject of *true* love.

In this analysis of the book of Ruth, we see a love story unfolding. It's primarily about God's love for His people, but it's also a story of the love between Ruth and Boaz.

Even if you don't love Jesus, be assured that you are loved more than you could ever imagine. "Jesus loves me" is a simple but profound statement. Jesus doesn't love you for the right decisions you make. He loves you, period. May that truth blow you away!

True Love

The couple we are looking at in this study are an example of true love. Their relationship beautifully demonstrated God's love for us, a love that is not contingent upon our obedience, our performance, or the exterior.

The Bible tells us that love never ends and never fails (1 Corinthians 13:8). True love entails a process that can't be rushed. That process is spiritual, relational, communal, sexual, and eternal, but God wants to start with the spirit. The order He has outlined for the process is spirit, then soul, and finally body.

Love is personal. Love pursued you and me even when we weren't looking for it. Therefore, love in its purest sense is not something we can fall out of, because we didn't fall into it.

So, why do people talk about "falling out" of love?

It's because they have hung their happiness on someone else. When their expectations are no longer met by that person, it's suddenly too difficult to stay together. But here's the thing: they were not really in *love* with the other person to begin with. They were in love with themselves. They never understood love from a biblical perspective.

Before we judge, however, let's be aware that you and I are prone to this type of love, too. We make love conditional, and our hearts and eyes wander. God's love is the only love that is not tainted by conditions or led by emotions.

Of course, being the object of His unconditional love does not mean we can live any way we please. I'm not promoting grace as a license to sin (see Romans 6:1–2).

But we must remember that nothing is more powerful than the unconditional love of God as expressed through Christ. When He died nearly two thousand years before we were born, Jesus rescued each of us from the eternal consequences of our future sin.

That all-important fact should grant us a whole new perspective on the words "I will love you forever, no matter what"!

Jesus' love was not contingent upon our obedience because we did not come out of the womb obeying. Nor was it contingent upon our performance, because we— especially we who were yet unborn—had not done anything to earn His love. Yet love pursued us.

Nor was His love contingent upon our exterior. He doesn't un-like us when we gain weight. He doesn't un-like us for having stretch marks. He doesn't un-like us for failing Him.

Friends, God loves us so much that He will not take His presence away from us. He will remove jobs, possessions, and people, but He won't remove Himself.

While God's love isn't conditional, it demands our highest commitment. We've seen this in Naomi's life. Remember how God was restoring Naomi to himself, even though she had been rejecting Ruth? Let's turn to Ruth chapter 3:

> One day Naomi said to Ruth, "My daughter, it's time that I found a permanent home for you, so that you will be provided for. Boaz is a close relative of ours, and he's been very kind by letting you gather grain with his young women. Tonight he will be winnowing barley at the threshing floor. Now do as I tell you—take a bath and put on perfume and dress in your nicest clothes. Then go to the threshing floor, but don't let Boaz see you until he has finished eating and drinking. Be sure to notice where he lies down; then go and uncover his feet and lie down there. He will tell you what to do."
>
> "I will do everything you say," Ruth replied. — **Ruth 3:1–5**

From this scripture, we can make three points about love. First, true love focuses on others.

Up to this point in the text, Naomi had thought about three people—not about Elimelech, Mahlon, or Kilion, but about *me, myself,* and *I.* But when we begin chapter 3, we finally see a change in perspective occurring: she was wondering about a permanent home for Ruth. At last, she was thinking about someone other than herself!

This captures Paul's teaching in Philippians 2:4, where he says, "Don't look out only for your own interests, but take an interest in others, too." When two people come together and try to out-serve each other, they both get loved.

Authentic love cares for the needs of others in the same way God cares for us. He was perfect within Himself—holy, loving, and joyful. Yet when He saw our condition, He left glory and came to save us—that's what it means to be other-centered, or selfless, instead of self-centered. It appears Naomi was finally showing this other-centered love instead of only loving herself.

Yet commentators may disagree on Naomi's motives. Was she truly caring for Ruth, or was she still looking after her own interests?

I would suggest that her heart was changing because she'd seen Ruth come back with a bucketful of barley. She'd seen God's *checed*—His lovingkindness, faithfulness, and goodness.

Playing Matchmaker

Now the picture gets a little dicey, as it seems Naomi was doing a bit of matchmaking! In the passage of Scripture above, it sounds as if she was giving Ruth tips on how to get herself a man.

But before we even begin to discuss whether a woman should approach a man, we must recall three facts:

First, Ruth was a Moabite woman, and Moabite women were notorious for using their bodies to get the men of Israel to walk away from the faith Numbers 25:1-3.

Secondly, the origin of Moab was an incestuous relationship between Lot and his oldest daughter (Genesis 19:30-38).

Thirdly, for an Israelite man, Boaz, to marry a Moabite woman would make him a social outcast.

In short, the stage was set for a beautifully unlikely love story, worthy of a Hollywood romance the likes of *Love and Basketball, Brown Sugar,* or *Pretty Woman.* Aware of the possibility suddenly before Ruth, Naomi offered her daughter-in-law five tips on how to get herself a husband:

- Take a bath and put on some perfume. (Men appreciate that.)
- Put on some nice clothes.
- Wait for him to eat and take a nap.
- Sneak into his room.
- Uncover his feet.

What exactly is happening here?

The first possibility is that Ruth is being told to *seduce to succeed.*

Seducing to Succeed?

Some of us might look at this text and say, "Well, Naomi encouraged Ruth to seduce him." And some women do teach others to operate in this way: "We need to use what we've got! Men have been doing it for years—now it's our turn!"

Sadly, many women indeed take this route to get a man. They show lots of skin, are sexually aggressive, and reject modesty. It has become the norm in our culture. In fact, sexual aggression and promiscuity are celebrated and labeled "empowering."

In such songs as Sza's "The Weekend," women are encouraged to level the playing field using their bodies. Though men won't argue with it one bit, because they benefit from this false sense of female empowerment, is this God's way? Does He want any of us manipulating others with our body in hopes of finding long-term fidelity? Of course not.

Is it possible Naomi thought Ruth didn't have morals because she was a Moabite woman? Perhaps she thought, "Well, I'm not asking Ruth to do anything she hasn't done before!"

Marriage is honorable and instituted by God, but the process of getting to the altar matters. I know people who have manipulated and schemed to get a spouse, only to be unsatisfied because marriage cannot satisfy the soul. Only God can do that.

Here is a saying that's as true as it is corny:

If you get the ring the wrong way,

In your marriage, you will pay.

If you use your body to get the ring, that's not faith. You are using something physical to enter into something God intended to be spiritual. *Seduce to succeed* is not God's way!

An Impatient Instigator?

Because Naomi was older and had no living husband or sons to care for her, she had a personal interest in being redeemed by Boaz. Whoever married Ruth would ultimately be responsible for Naomi, too. At least in part, therefore, Naomi wanted to be redeemed by Boaz because she knew he was a source of food. He was her kinsman-redeemer.

As a result, Naomi might not have expected Ruth to seduce Boaz, but was her advice nonetheless motivated by impatience? Not everyone goes the "seduce to succeed" route, but sometimes we do move prematurely.

A woman might be ready to drop a hint or two because the guy in whom she's interested hasn't approached her yet. Therefore, she tells somebody close to him that she finds him cute and ensures it gets back to him.

I am not saying women can't initiate friendship, but men and women alike need to check their hearts. They must ask themselves: "What is my motivation?"

At this point, we need to remember the words of the wise women in Song of Solomon:

> Promise me, O women of Jerusalem, by the gazelles and wild deer, **not to awaken love until the time is right.** —
> **Song of Solomon 2:7** *(emphasis added)*

Most of that book is written in the context of sexual love between a husband and wife, but the key principle is

"Be patient!" We are not to awaken love until the time is right.

And yes, our patience will be tested. We may have no patience left, but the Spirit does—and He will lead us into all truth. We don't have to manipulate things as Naomi might have done.

An Authentic Appeal?

Another possibility, and the most likely, is that Naomi knew the law and wanted Ruth to appeal to Boaz to be a man of God. Her instructions to Ruth simply could have been meant as guidelines for approaching Boaz in the most respectful way.

To be sure, Ruth was putting herself out there. She was essentially asking Boaz to marry her. Especially in our relatively disconnected society of atomized individuals, a man and a woman should discover each other through friendship prior to making the lifelong commitment to marriage. True love embraces total exposure as a gateway to authentic intimacy.

Marriage will expose many things, but in our modern culture we hide as much as we can until we get the ring. We hide the embarrassing details about ourselves because we think someone won't continue to love us when they see our flaws. We think the more a person knows us, the less likely he or she will be to love us, so we wear a mask.

But the gospel turns that on its head, doesn't it? Jesus knew all of your dirt and mine, yet still died for you and me. He knew the things your pastor doesn't know about you, things maybe even your spouse doesn't know about you, but He still chose you. Thus, we need to stop trying to conceal ourselves.

Ruth already knew Boaz was a kind man worthy of respect (Ruth 2:8–10, 2:20). For Boaz's part, he knew she was a hard worker (Ruth 2:6), humble (Ruth 2:10), and compassionate (Ruth 2:11–12). And her proposal itself told him a lot about her moral character.

An Other-Centered Proposal

In the case of Ruth and Boaz, however, the process of cultivating honest and lasting love also involved a bold move on her part:

So, she went down to the threshing floor that night and followed the instructions of her mother-in-law.

After Boaz had finished eating and drinking and was in good spirits, he lay down at the far end of the pile of grain and went to sleep. Then Ruth came quietly, uncovered his feet, and lay down. Around midnight Boaz suddenly woke up and turned over. He was surprised to find a woman lying at his feet! "Who are you?" he asked.

"I am your servant Ruth," she replied. "Spread the corner of your covering over me, for you are my family redeemer."

*"The Lord bless you, my daughter!" Boaz exclaimed. "You are showing even more family loyalty now than you did before, for you have not gone after a younger man, whether rich or poor. Now don't worry about a thing, my daughter. I will do what is necessary, for everyone in town knows you are a virtuous woman." — **Ruth 3:6–11***

At that time, when a man wanted to let a woman know of his commitment, he would take his garment and put the edge of it over her. This signified being connected to her and his desire to cover her. This custom was alluded to in Ezekiel 16:8:

> And when I passed by again, I saw that you were old enough for love. So, I wrapped my cloak around you to cover your nakedness and declared my marriage vows. I made a covenant with you, says the Sovereign LORD, and you became mine.

In Jewish culture, the cloak represented a covering that was not supposed to be removed. The only thing that would cause you to remove the covering was death.

Ruth was not coming at Boaz merely looking for a boyfriend. She was coming at him seeking *commitment*. And it was an important commitment. The garment was connected to him, and he used it to signify he wanted to bring her in as his own.

Thus, when Ruth said, "Spread the corner of your covering of me," she invoked the same concept of commitment, responsibility, and protection to which Boaz referred when he spoke previously of the wings of God: "May the LORD, the God of Israel, under whose wings you have come to take refuge…" (Ruth 2:12).

Remember, Boaz ultimately points us to Jesus. Therefore, when Ruth was saying, "Cover me," she was also saying, "You are my kinsman-redeemer—so redeem me!" This was tantamount to a proposal, but she was appealing to the law of her time and she was doing so in faith. True, she had deviated a little from Naomi's instructions. Naomi had told her to take a bath, put on her best clothes, uncover his feet, let him eat and sleep, and then wait. But Ruth got there early, and when Boaz woke up, she appealed to him to be a man of God by taking up his duty to embrace the family of his deceased relative, Elimelech.

Ruth's proposal was countercultural because in their culture, women never proposed to men. The younger certainly didn't propose to the older, and the servant didn't propose to the owner.

Moreover, Ruth was not thinking only about herself. She knew that if she got married, Naomi, her mother-in-law, would have a home. Love is always other-centered.

Again, this points us to the gospel, because Jesus defied norms and demonstrated and other-centeredness when He pursued us. God was thus at work in Ruth's actions.

A Righteous Response

Boaz was the kinsman-redeemer responsible for taking care of his deceased relative's family, but this situation was atypical because Ruth was a Moabite woman. He had the option to reject her—especially considering her countercultural approach—but he did not.

Again, Boaz pointed us to Christ, the sinless God marrying a sinful bride. Like Ruth, we were poor in spirit and brought nothing to the table except our sin.

Ruth was appealing to Boaz with a heart and spirit of faith. And Boaz, for his part, was floored by Ruth's demonstration of an other-centered approach to love. Remember how bitter Naomi had been? She hadn't even wanted her daughter-in-law to accompany her, and she had hardly spoken one word to Ruth. Yet Ruth had put herself out there. That was love. Furthermore, she had placed herself in danger by venturing out late at night. That, too, was love.

When Boaz noticed her, he exclaimed:

> *The LORD bless you, my daughter! You are showing even more family loyalty now than you did before, for you have not gone after a younger man, whether rich or poor. Now don't worry about a thing, my daughter. I will do what is necessary, for everyone in town knows you are a virtuous woman.* — **Ruth 3:10–11**

Boaz said this second act of Ruth's was even greater than the first. Ruth was young, while Boaz was an older man. He was a bit staggered that she would even want him. He said, "You know what? You could have gone after someone younger, with more money."

Ruth's character exceeded even her physical beauty. Boaz had heard about her character, especially how she had left Moab to take care of her mother-in-law. This would be the greater testimony in the end, because one day her looks would fade. That's why we read in Proverbs:

Charm is deceitful, and beauty does not last; but a woman who fears the LORD will be greatly praised. — ***Proverbs 31:30***

A God-fearing woman should be pursued. Ruth deserved to be pursued. *You* should be pursued, too.

A Glitch in the Process?

"But while it's true that I am one of your family redeemers," Boaz said, "there is another man who is more closely related to you than I am. Stay here tonight, and in the morning I will talk to him. If he is willing to redeem you, very well. Let him marry you. But if he is not willing, then as surely as the LORD lives, I will redeem you myself! Now lie down here until morning." — ***Ruth 3:12-13***

Ruth had put a lot of effort into this encounter. She'd had a bath. She was wearing her best perfume and her best clothes. She was also appealing to the law. She wanted her mother-in-law to be taken care of. In short, she was asking Boaz to be the man of God she knew he was.

After all that work, Boaz was saying, "I feel for you, Ruth, but there is somebody more closely related to you than I am, someone else who could step in and redeem you."

Can you imagine how Ruth must have felt? Rejected, disappointed, and humiliated? But such a response leaves out one crucial fact:

We are not in control.

Ruth put herself out there, but because he was an upright man, Boaz wanted to go through the proper process. Ruth may have been appealing to the law, but the law said the closest relative had first dibs. (Thankfully, we're not held to that rule today!) Though Boaz wanted her, a man of God follows God even when it hurts.

If this book of the Bible were a Hollywood production, it would have been the end of the movie. Ruth would have her cloak on, Boaz would sport a great goatee, and they would walk off into the sunset. Then we'd hear Bruno Mars in the background: "Because you are amazing just the way you are!"[9]

But our story doesn't end like that. In Ruth chapter 4, we see Boaz being a real man. We don't hear any more of Ruth for the rest of the chapter because Boaz was taking the lead. At this point, Ruth could do nothing but wait.

Built on Patience

Ever since the days of Genesis chapter 3, women have been tempted to lead men in relationships (see Genesis 3:16). Women are tempted not to let men be men and not to trust God's process regarding marital commitment.

Ruth might have protested, "I put myself out here, I've worn my best cloak, and now you're telling me there's somebody closer whom I might need to marry? No way! You are going to marry me right now, Boaz!"

Instead, she had to fall back and let him take the lead. She had to accept the temporary vulnerability of her situation.

Love requires vulnerability, doesn't it? We can't live with an emotional Fort Knox around us.

Moreover, Boaz in his role here was pointing us toward the true redeemer of humanity, Jesus Christ. As Boaz owned the field and took the initiative in Ruth's redemption, Jesus owned the earth and took the initiative in enacting our salvation. As Ruth had to submit to Boaz's lead in her situation, we must submit to the fact that only Jesus possesses the power and authority to redeem us.

> *So Ruth lay at Boaz's feet until the morning, but she got up before it was light enough for people to recognize each other. For Boaz had said, "No one must know that a woman was here at the threshing floor." Then Boaz said to her, "Bring your cloak and spread it out." He measured six scoops of barley into the cloak and placed it on her back. Then he returned to the town.* **— Ruth 3:14–15**

Boaz was honoring her. Nothing sexual happened.

> *When Ruth went back to her mother-in-law, Naomi asked, "What happened, my daughter?"* **— Ruth 3:16**

Naomi might as well have asked Ruth, "Girl, what happened last night?"

> *Ruth told Naomi everything Boaz had done for her, and she added, "He gave me these six scoops of barley and*

said, 'Don't go back to your mother-in-law empty-handed.'"

*Then Naomi said to her, "Just be patient, my daughter, until we hear what happens. The man won't rest until he has settled things today." — **Ruth 3:16–18***

Ruth and Boaz were the poster couple for people of character. Ruth was young and evidently strong, judging by the weight she could carry on her back for long distances. Boaz was an older man. They weren't your typical glamor duo, like Jay-Z and Beyoncé, but they were people of solid character. True love is built on character rather than on physical attraction.

I don't know of any couple who stayed together because they were cute, but I do know couples who have had long-lasting marriages because of their character.

However, in all there were three love stories at play here: Ruth and Naomi, Ruth and Boaz, and a third—God and His people.

God's Love Story

Of course, it's the third story that matters most to us. This is the story of God's love for His runaway bride, the story that began in Genesis. It was in a garden that the bride and groom ran away after they took the fruit, but it was in the garden of Gethsemane that Jesus redeemed humankind.

God went after His runaway bride—that's you and me. And if we come to Him, we will not leave empty-handed. The moment we put our faith in Him, we will leave filled with the Holy Spirit. With that in mind, here are three challenges for us:

- Rest in the fact that God loves us *because He is love* and not because of what we do.
- Ask God to cultivate a selfless, other-centered attitude in us. Do we have a sense of entitlement of which we need to repent? Do we avoid serving others, or the church, because it's all about us?
- Share the greatest love story in history with someone. Our love for one another will prove to the world that we are Jesus' disciples (John 13:35).

No matter how dark—or pristine—we may think our past is right now, we all need redemption through Jesus. God's love for us is the only true love.

What Is Love?

Notice that through the unfolding of this love story, we find out what love is and what love is not. Nowhere in Scripture is love described as a feeling. Love is not a feeling, because we will not always feel love.

Love, in essence, encompasses three things:

1. **Love is a person.** First John 4:7–8 tells us that "God is **love**."
2. **Love is a choice.** John 14:15 tells that if we **love** Christ, we will obey Him.

3. **Love is an action.** Romans 5:8 tells us that "God demonstrated his **love** while we were still sinners" when Christ died for us.

Knowing love is a person, a choice, and an action enables us to love people even when we don't feel like it. He doesn't need to renew His love for us. Rather, we need to renew our love for Him who redeems us.

WORKBOOK

Chapter 4 Questions

Question: How have you encountered the love of God? How have you experienced Jesus' love?

_____

_____

_____

_____

_____

_____

_____

_____

_____

_____

_____

Question: How do you demonstrate an attitude of faith on a daily basis in your loving human relationships?

How can you approach your relationship with God with the faith and trust His love deserves?

_____

_____

_____

_____

_____

_____

_____

_____

_____

_____

_____

Question: What costs have you or those close to you paid for love? What are some specific instances in which you've had to be patient to show God's love to someone? What was the payoff?

_____

_____

_____

_____

_____

_____

_____

_____

_____

_____

_____

_____

Action: Approach God each day with a renewed attitude of faith and love. Reflect on His love as you experience it throughout the day, and show His love to everyone you encounter. Then share the story of His love with someone who needs to hear it, as the Spirit leads you.

Chapter 4 Notes

_____

_____

_____

_____

_____

_____

_____

_____

_____

_____

_____

_____

_____

_____

_____

_____

_____

_____

_____

_____

_____

_____

CHAPTER FIVE

Redemption and Renewed Hope

No matter how financially responsible you are, or how good your credit score is, you may be in debt.

On the one hand, most of us owe someone something. Each of us likely has at least one regular bill, which is a form of debt, we need to pay.

Beyond the financial and the mundane, moreover, you and I also owe God. When He purchased us with the life of His Son, He set us free from the *penalty*, the *power*, and the *presence* of sin. The renewal we need begins with the canceling of our eternal debt—not the debts of which our creditors keep reminding us.

Right now, if we are in Christ, we are only experiencing freedom from the *penalty* and *power* of sin. But one day, when Jesus returns, we will also be saved from the *presence* of sin. Paul put it like this:

> *For everyone has sinned; we all fall short of God's glorious standard. Yet God, in his grace, freely makes us right in his sight. He did this through Christ Jesus when he freed*

us from the penalty for our sins. For God presented Jesus as the sacrifice for sin. People are made right with God when they believe that Jesus sacrificed his life, shedding his blood. This sacrifice shows that God was being fair when he held back and did not punish those who sinned in times past, for he was looking ahead and including them in what he would do in this present time. God did this to demonstrate his righteousness, for he himself is fair and just, and he makes sinners right in his sight when they believe in Jesus. — **Romans 3:23-26**

That's what redemption is about. The word 'redeem' simply means to buy back. But when we talk about redemption in the biblical sense, it's more than being bought back. It's about cancelling an eternal debt permanently.

You and I can't save ourselves. We bring nothing to the table except our sin. If we could save ourselves, why would we need Christ? The renewed life begins when we accept the unearned, unconditional grace that He offers us.

For a life to be renewed, the process needs to go deeper than our external circumstances. Only the gospel of Christ can renew us from within. Then we can live with the eternal perspective that only God can provide.

I teach my children theological terms from time to time. Their first such word was 'propitiation.' Now when I ask them, "What does *propitiate* mean?" they tell me it means "to satisfy."

Then I ask, "Okay, and how did Jesus satisfy?"

I turn to them with my arms outstretched and explain, "When Jesus died on the cross to reconcile God and man, He *satisfied* God's wrath. He bought us back. That's the story of the Bible."

Redemption is the overarching message of the Bible. It's a story that shines through sixty-six books and more than thirty thousand verses. The Bible tells us how God redeems, how He pursues, and how He transforms fallen humanity by His love. Jesus cancels our sin debt so we might live in Him.

Transformation in Christ

What does it mean to be in Christ?

There is a significant difference between being in Christ and simply going to church. To be in Christ means our life is transformed by who He is and what He has done. It's doesn't rest on the faith of those around us— we need to own it. When we stand before Him, we will have to give an account for how we have lived.

Do we live with that understanding?

Satan, the accuser, wants to accuse God of not being just. "Just look at all the sin in the Old Testament that He did nothing about! How could God blame you for that?" Satan might ask.

And God could respond, "Oh yes, I did do something about it. I carried out the judgment on My Son."

The Old Testament has all kinds of drama in it. You might have wondered how God actually could have *used* some of those people! The fact that He did should give us hope. If God can use prostitutes, adulterers, extortionists, and thieves, He really *is* a Redeemer!

A True Redeemer

God allowed a Moabite woman to be redeemed despite the fact that His people, the Israelites, were discouraged from associating with Moabites. Though Boaz wasn't Jesus, his example of accepting outsiders pointed the way to Jesus.

Ruth asked Boaz to fulfill the role of her redeemer, but as we've read, it turned out another relative was next in line. However, Naomi reassured Ruth that Boaz would sort everything out (Ruth 3:18). And indeed, he did—though the initial response of the other relative was not what Boaz or Ruth wanted to hear:

> *Boaz went to the town gate and took a seat there. Just then the family redeemer he had mentioned came by, so Boaz called out to him, "Come over here and sit down, friend. I want to talk to you." So they sat down together. Then Boaz called ten leaders from the town and asked them to sit as witnesses. And Boaz said to the family redeemer, "You know Naomi, who came back from Moab. She is selling the land that belonged to our relative Elimelech. I thought I should speak to you about it so that you can redeem it if you wish. If you want the land, then buy it here in the presence of these witnesses. But if you don't want it, let me know right away, because I am next in line to redeem it after you."*
>
> *The man replied, "All right, I'll redeem it." —* ***Ruth 4:1–4***

In Ruth chapter 4, we see the work of the redeemer. Ruth had indicated she wanted to be redeemed, but it was the redeemer who did all the work.

We must also examine this story through an eternal, spiritual lens: What are some characteristics of a redeemer?

In the four verses above, we find six such characteristics:

1. The redeemer initiates redemption.

Boaz makes the first move, and if we go back to Genesis 3:9, we see that the first evangelist was God Himself when He asked, "Adam, where are you?" The moment Adam sinned, God came looking for him!

It is a good thing the Redeemer makes the first move, because if it were up to us, we would never get redeemed. It's unlikely that we would spontaneously say, "You know what? I'm tired of doing things my way. I've decided to take the initiative and give up my way of doing things!"

The Bible is clear that nobody is saved unless the Spirit draws him or her (John 6:44). Thus, God always takes the initiative.

2. The redeemer publicly displays his love for those needing redemption.

In Ruth 4:2, we notice Boaz has brought many witnesses together. This was common in Israelite culture, He was trying to redeem this woman, and he wanted people to see his love for her.

Moreover, this public display points us to Jesus. Didn't He display His love on the cross? Wasn't He publicly ridiculed? Didn't they scream "Crucify him!" and didn't He suffer publicly because He loved us?

Jesus was not ashamed of us. The crown of thorns they put on Him was meant for you and me. Yet He endured public scorn because of God's glory and His love for us.

3. The redeemer is intimately aware of those needing redemption.

In Ruth 4:3, you will see Boaz knew Ruth's history. Boaz knew that Moabite women were typically known for sleeping around with the men of Israel. He was aware of their reputation, but he still wanted to redeem this Moabite woman.

Again, his behavior points us to Jesus. Jesus knows our deepest secrets. He has seen all the dark corners of our hearts. This darkness doesn't change His love for you, but you need to give it over to Him. You can't fix it yourself. Redemption is the work of the Redeemer.

4. The redeemer has the means to redeem.

In Ruth 4:4, Boaz invites the other kinsman to buy the land in the presence of witnesses and adds, "If you won't do it, I will." In other words, "I have enough money to buy this land and to take care of both Ruth and Naomi."

In the Old Testament, priests would sacrifice lambs to atone for people's sins. That was why John the Baptist said of Jesus: "Look! the Lamb of God who takes away the sin of the world!" (John 1:29).

Boaz points us to Christ—the only One who had the means to pay the debt that we owe. This is why Paul writes to the church at Colossae that not only did Christ die for us, but in doing so He also paid and cancelled the eternal debt we owe (Colossians 2:14). We don't have enough moral capital ourselves because God's standard is perfection. Our own bank account is bankrupt. Not one of us measures up to God's standard. We failed God's test, for Jesus said, "But you are to be perfect, even as your Father in heaven is perfect" (Matthew 5:48).

We'd be doomed if Christ the Redeemer hadn't made a way for us to be made right with God! As Romans chapter 6 teaches us, we are saved only by the grace of God manifested in Jesus:

So, you also should consider yourselves to be dead to the power of sin and alive to God through Christ Jesus. ... Now you do those things that lead to holiness and result in eternal life. For the wages of sin is death, but the free gift of God is eternal life through Christ Jesus our Lord.
— ***Romans 6:11, 6:22–23***

God's redemption turns our guilt into innocence. He tells the guilty person, "You are innocent because I did your time for you. I paid the price to buy you back." He bought us back from the kingdom of darkness and welcomed us into His kingdom.

5. The redeemer redeems simply because he loves.

Boaz was putting forth a lot of effort, and from a human perspective, what was he really getting out of it? He was the one who was spending the money, and he was the one who was approaching the other relative to negotiate. But he was motivated to these actions by his love for Ruth.

Similarly, Jesus gave everything for us simply because He loved us. In the ordinary scheme of things, there would be no benefit for Christ to sacrifice His life. But in the eternal scheme of things, He endured the cross, the scorn, and the shame because it put Him at the right hand of the Father (Hebrews 12:2). Jesus lived with and embodies this eternal perspective.

6. The redeemer desires to redeem us.

That may sound simple, but it's truly profound.

Boaz said, "Look, if you're going to redeem her, then redeem her, but if not, I'm next in line." In effect, he was saying, "I want her. I want the responsibility. I want to do whatever it takes to redeem her. I want to take in both Ruth and Naomi."

What does that mean for us? It means that Jesus desires to redeem us!

A terrible lie that so many people mouth is: "Nobody wants me!" Jesus wants us, flaws and all. We don't bring anything to the table, nor do we have to make ourselves more presentable in order to be accepted by Him. The

Lord personifies love, peace, and patience—and He *loves* us.

If we are disciples of Christ, we need to tell people who feel unloved, "Not only does Jesus want you, but together we can share in the love and redemption that He brings." We can tell people whom we barely know that we love them and want to see them in the Kingdom. We can tell them we want to worship Christ with them.

There is no person who is too hard for God to redeem—including you. Perhaps you are saying, "Jerome, you don't know my story. You don't know all the things I've done. You don't know the people I've hurt. You don't know how I've been hurt...."

You are right, I don't know. But I know who cares. And that's all *you* need to know at this point. Your sin doesn't disqualify you from grace, because that's why grace exists.

On the other side of the coin, don't let your *righteousness* keep you from grace, either. Everyone needs renewal—everyone needs the Redeemer! It's not about an accumulation of good deeds. It's about placing faith in the Redeemer.

The Fine Print

Now that we have looked at the characteristics of a redeemer, let's continue the story from Ruth 4:5:

Then Boaz told him, "Of course, your purchase of the land from Naomi also requires that you marry Ruth, the Moabite widow. That way she can have children who will carry

on her husband's name and keep the land in the family."
— Ruth 4:5

Now Boaz was getting down to the fine print. The other relative had said cheerfully, "I will redeem the land," but now Boaz was pointing out that there was a bit more to it than the other man had perhaps realized.

"Then I can't redeem it," the family redeemer replied, "because this might endanger my estate. You redeem the land; I cannot do it." — Ruth 4:6

What has happened in these two verses? In verse 4 he had said, "I will redeem it!" while in verse 6 he was saying, "I can't redeem it."

Commentators have different views on his change of mind, and there may be more than one explanation. One possibility is the financial aspect. With his own family to consider, the other kinsman couldn't afford to take on any new members.

Another possibility was that if he *did* redeem her, Ruth would get some of his estate when he died. And maybe he didn't want a Moabite woman to get any of *his* money.

There certainly could have been a financial struggle, but remember how quickly he offered to take up the deal in the first place? The issue was not *only* money. Once he found out about Ruth, he backed out. He was now presented with the issue of this Moabite woman and what it might do to his reputation.

What was Ruth doing during this exchange? She was waiting patiently, as instructed. "Trust me," Boaz had said, "and I'll get this sorted out."

Again, this situation points us to Jesus, who also says to us, "I am coming back, trust Me."

Romans chapter 5 talks about the difference between the first Adam and the second Adam, who was Christ (Romans 5:12–19). This is what Christ says to you: "The first Adam brought death, but I bring life. I know all of your deepest and darkest secrets, yet I have sufficient grace to cover all of them. I still want you."

Similarly, and unlike the other potential redeemer in the story of Ruth, Boaz said, "I have enough. I know her past, but I want her anyway." Again, Boaz points us to Christ.

We may not be perfect, and our pasts may be checkered, yet Christ still died for each of us.

Here's the ironic part: the other relative declined to redeem Ruth because he wanted to protect his name. When you want to protect your name, however, you miss out on the Messiah. When the other relative declined Ruth, he didn't realize she would one day have a baby whose lineage would lead to Christ.

This relative is never mentioned again in Scripture.

Do you see the point? The very thing you think is going to save you ultimately costs you. Unless it's Jesus.

A Transfer of Ownership

Because our plans often do not align with God's will for His kingdom, it sometimes seems as if God might crush our dreams. And sometimes, in fact, He does. Take these examples, for instance:

"I *so* wanted to play D1 basketball. But I tore my ACL and it was the best thing that happened to me. When it happened my dream was destroyed, but God was up to something."

"I thought I was going to be a lawyer. I went through all those years of school, and then God had me become a missionary in Africa. I've got all this education, but I'm not using any of it!"

The fine print of being a disciple of Christ means we die to our pride. *We cannot build God's kingdom if we are not willing to destroy our own.*

Are we trying to protect our name, as Ruth's other relative was?

Are we avoiding some of the people God wants to place in our life because we are afraid of what those associations will do to our reputation in the eyes of other people? When we keep the lid on our reputation, it may cause us to miss out.

To be honest, ministry is not the profession I would have chosen for myself. I didn't plan to be speaking in front of a couple hundred people on Sundays, knowing that some of them weren't going to listen. I can't tell you what my plan was, but thank God for grace!

And thank God for His sovereignty. Thank God, I was not in control. Now I wouldn't trade my life for the world. I get to preach the gospel and see people saved, and I get to be a missionary to my city.

Boaz was showing us the renewed life when he put the needs of Ruth and Naomi above his own. As Paul would write to church at Philippi, "Be humble, thinking of others as better than yourselves" (Philippians 2:3).

When we begin to live that way, everyone is served and our communities will be transformed!

For instance, did you know that if a small percentage of the body of Christ gave financially—not all of us, just a percentage—we could drastically impact poverty? Yet we cling tightly to our money because we believe it belongs to us. Could we be trying to build our own kingdom while claiming His?

We need to destroy the false kingdoms of our personal will and surrender fully to God's will. This is a struggle, but it's worth the fight. When we destroy our will, we are willingly transferring ownership of our lives to God and allowing the Redeemer to do His work.

Even when our circumstances don't make sense, or when it seems the will of God directly opposes ours, He is working in our lives. If we remain in Him, our dream should align with His will. That's why the Bible says He will give us the desires of our heart—if we desire and delight in Him (see Psalm 37:4).

The Three T's

*Now in those days it was the custom in Israel for anyone transferring a right of purchase to remove his sandal and hand it to the other party. This publicly validated the transaction. So the other family redeemer drew off his sandal as he said to Boaz, "You buy the land." — **Ruth 4:7-8***

Thus, the custom in Israel when handing over the right of a kinsman-redeemer was to surrender one's sandal and say, essentially, "Buy it for yourself."

The renewed life begins with a transfer of ownership. Back then a legal transaction was finalized by this symbolic gesture. The passing of the sandal certified that Boaz now owned the land.

Again, we are like Ruth. We're outsiders with immense needs. And when we trust Christ, we sign over the deed to our life.

When we come into possession of a building, as the new owner, we have the right to do what we want with it. Knowing this, have you signed over the deed of your life to Jesus, so He can do what He wants with you?

Perhaps you are wondering, "Well, how would I know?" The answer lies in three T's—trust, transformation, and trust (again):

The first T is the trust that occurs at *salvation*. "Lord, I come." Some of us got saved in a traditional church setting. But however we came to Jesus, trust came first. We must trust in His finished work on the cross on our behalf.

The second T is *transformation*, or *sanctification* in theological speak. This is the process of God making us more like Him. Paul calls this being "conformed to the image" of Christ (Romans 8:9 ESV).

The third T is trust in the promise of *glorification*. We trust that Jesus is coming back for us and we will experience His kingdom for all of eternity.

What's my point? It's not whether we trusted Him at age twelve—it's whether we're still trusting Him *now*.

Salvation isn't a past event but a present reality of ongoing gratitude, maturity, service, and love for what Christ has done for us.

The Deed to Our Lives

You and I had a deed to our lives, and on it was written what we believed about money, family, work, church, and God. The deed dictated how we approached relationships, how we approached sex, and how we approached other men and women.

I thought I owned the deed to my life. I considered my perspective to be the truth.

However, when I signed over the deed to my life, I didn't just sign over a small piece of my being. I signed over my thoughts, my heart, my emotions, my speech— all of me.

But when we sign over our deed to God, everything changes. God says, "This is how you used to think about women, but now I want you to think about women in all purity. And I'll help you get there.

"This is what you used to think about money, but now I want you to live generously. You used to think church was optional, but I saved you out of the world and *into* the church. Now live joyfully for Me.

"You used to think you could make yourself right with Me. But now that you understand that you can't, live in grace."

When we sign over our deed, God begins to transform us. But would this be obvious to other people? An Irish evangelist named Gypsy Smith once said, "There are five Gospels—Matthew, Mark, Luke, John, and the Christian—but most people never read the first four."[10] The point is, we are the only gospel some people will have.

What gospel is our life preaching at work? Are we joining in the gossip about the boss? Are we talking about how we got lit last night? Do we care about the souls of those who are observing us?

"Well," you might be saying in some embarrassment, "I guess I did join in on the gossip at work the other day. Have I totally blown my testimony?"

Absolutely not. Love Jesus enough to say to your co-workers, "Look, I haven't been honoring the Lord well before you. But I want to apologize for not being a good witness as a Christian. I want to tell you there is something called grace, which is why I'm able to come here and admit I was laughing about being intoxicated and joining in the office gossip.

"As a matter of fact, I was taking joy in what the Bible calls sin. I was even tweeting about it! But because of this grace, I can come to you and ask for your forgiveness."

Then tell them you are going to do your best to honor God. Tell them you know you're no better than they are, but you're a recipient of grace and they can be, too. God is our Redeemer!

When you go back to people and admit your shortcomings, you are showing Christian character. People may still decide to go their own way, but you have declared you belong to God and He holds the deed to your life.

Responding with Hope

Since the fall of man, too many people have chosen to go their own way instead. Some of the people in the story of Ruth were no different.

> Then Boaz said to the elders and to the crowd standing around, "You are witnesses that today I have bought from Naomi all the property of Elimelech, Kilion, and Mahlon. And with the land I have acquired Ruth, the Moabite widow of Mahlon, to be my wife. This way she can have a son to carry on the family name of her dead husband and to inherit the family property here in his hometown. You are all witnesses today." — **Ruth 4:9–10**

Notice that in these two verses, Boaz named everyone in the story except the other potential redeemer and Orpah. Why?

Because both of them chose their own way. One said he wanted to save his name—and lost it instead. The other decided to play it safe and stay in Moab.

> Then the elders and all the people standing in the gate replied, "We are witnesses! May the LORD make this woman who is coming into your home like Rachel and Leah, from whom all the nation of Israel descended! May you prosper in Ephrathah and be famous in Bethlehem. And may the LORD give you descendants by this young woman who will be like those of our ancestor Perez, the son of Tamar and Judah." — **Ruth 4:9–10**

After the agreement was signed, everyone witnessed this true love. But what did Leah, Rachel, and Tamar have to do with it? Where did they come from?

Rachel and Leah's story was told in Genesis 29–31. You may recall that Jacob was tricked by his uncle Laban, and he ended up marrying Leah.

Now, Leah didn't have what we might call great "facial artistry." So, Jacob didn't really "feel" Leah like he did her sister. Rachel, however, was gorgeous.

Yet the lineage that led to Christ came through Leah, not Rachel. She gave Jacob four sons, and the fourth she named Judah, which meant "praise." Judah became part of another story, which began in Genesis chapter 38.

In that chapter, we meet Tamar. Tamar's husband was a wicked man named Er, who died. Then Judah, who was Tamar's father-in-law, told his son Onan, who would be the next in line to marry her, that he needed to provide children for Tamar. The Bible tells us, however, that whenever they were intimate, Onan would withdraw.

Therefore, Tamar was never able to have a baby. In that culture, it was significantly important for women to have children—so Tamar decided to take matters into her own hands by dressing like a prostitute.

She covered her face with a veil, and sat by the roadside. Judah was going down the road and ended up sleeping with his daughter-in-law, thinking she was a prostitute (Genesis 38:14–15)!

Tamar gave birth to Zerah and Perez. Boaz came through the line of Perez.

Why would God link up with such detestable people?

Because He links up with us. These broken people were the ones Christ came to redeem. Just look at the family tree of those God chose to use! The renewed life is about living lavishly in God's grace. And don't miss who did all the work: The Redeemer! Jesus did the heavy lifting.

How can we respond to the work of our Redeemer?

- We can *remember* His work by meditating on His Word and listening to His voice. When we feel as if the pain is not worth it, we need to remember the Redeemer.
- We can *reveal* His work in how we live, wherever we are and in every season of life.
- We can *repeat* His work by sharing it with others, rather than keeping the good news to ourselves.
- We can *rest* in His work. He has made us right with Himself. It was not something we could have done by ourselves.

So many Christians don't stay the course because of pain in their lives. They get worn down by trying to build both their kingdom and God's. We can't build both.

But Paul said, "I have fought the good fight, I have finished the race, and I have remained faithful" (2 Timothy 4:7). When we fight the good fight and remain faithful, we can have the renewed hope that God is our Redeemer all the time—not just at the moment we transferred ownership.

Boaz, too, was upright and faithful. His dealings were honorable and astute. And now he finally had his bride, Ruth. The stage was set for the incredible end to a compelling love story.

WORKBOOK

Chapter 5 Questions

Question: When has another person acted as a redeemer in your life? How was that experience similar to, and different from, your spiritual redemption by Christ?

_____

_____

_____

_____

_____

_____

_____

_____

_____

_____

_____

Question: What does it mean for you to be in Christ? How has He transformed your life? In what areas or ways do you need to let His power shape your life even more fully?

_____

_____

_____

_____

_____

_____

_____

_____

_____

_____

Question: When have you passed up opportunities to extend God's love to others to protect your reputation? What were the consequences? How would you act differently if you had the chance for a do-over?

_____

_____

_____

_____

_____

_____

_____

_____

_____

Action: Surrender the deed to your life to your Redeemer! Place your trust and hope where it belongs, in Jesus Christ. Let Him work His transforming, sanctifying power in every area of your life and reach others through you.

Chapter 5 Notes

CHAPTER SIX

Purpose Renewed

Perhaps our lives would be better off if we spent more time dwelling on death. Gloomy, right?

But consider: apart from the imaginary violence that pervades our entertainment, death holds a certain taboo quality in today's youth- and youthfulness-crazed culture. However, serious contemplation of death can help renew our appreciation for life and the choices we make. The reality of death underscores the fact that our decisions always affect others—resulting in either collateral damage or collateral blessings.

Talking about death might seem morbid, but at one time this was the popular way to share the gospel with someone. "How are you doing? Where would you go if you died today?" We used to say this to people who didn't even know our last name! Thank God that our outreach efforts have matured from asking someone we barely know about their demise.

Even so, if we're honest, the prospect and ultimate certainty of physical death have a way of renewing our perspective on life *right now.*

A psalm I love contains these words: "So teach us *to number our days,* that we may get a heart of wisdom" (Psalm 90:12 ESV, emphasis added). Another says: "LORD, remind me how brief my time on earth will be. Remind me that my days are numbered—how fleeting my life is" (Psalm 39:4).

Whenever I minister to men's groups, one thing I always tell them is that it doesn't matter how they started. It matters how they finish. That's what they will be remembered for.

Did they finish their lives womanizing? Did they finish by abandoning their children? Did they finish by never taking responsibility? Or will they be able to say they have finished well by the grace of God?

In other words, before we make any decision, let's think about the impact it will have in our life and in the lives of others. Let me ask you: *What epitaph would you like on your tombstone?*

The follow-up question is: *And would that inscription be accurate?* The decisions we make in life do matter. No one is going to live perfectly—that's why we need grace—but we do need to think about the legacy we're going to leave.

A Legacy of Grace

So, Boaz took Ruth into his home, and she became his wife. When he slept with her, the LORD enabled her to be-

come pregnant, and she gave birth to a son. Then the
women of the town said to Naomi, "Praise the LORD, who
has now provided a redeemer for your family! May this
child be famous in Israel. May he restore your youth and
care for you in your old age. For he is the son of your
daughter-in-law who loves you and has been better to
you than seven sons!" — Ruth 4:13-15

Boaz had no idea how God was going to use him as a redeemer. He had no idea what a powerful legacy he would leave for generations to come.

Remember, Ruth had been barren for a decade. As we learned in Ruth chapter 1, she was widowed after ten years of marriage but had borne no children. She wanted a child but never had one.

Boaz had gone to the other kinsman-redeemer, who was unnamed, and they agreed that Boaz would redeem the land after all, because the other man didn't want to take Ruth and Naomi as part of the package. After the deed had been signed over, Ruth and Boaz got married.

Over the span of four chapters, bad decisions were made and three people died, leaving three widows. But the story ends with a new marriage and a new life.

This is what Jesus does in our lives! We come as barren people, but we leave with much more. Ten years of mistakes were undone in one moment, because that's what happens the moment we trust in Jesus.

We go from being children of the enemy to royal sons and daughters of God! We become Spirit-filled, joyful, victorious kids of the King who are no longer lonely.

As we reflect on the story of Ruth in its entirety, we see the legacy God gives us by His grace. The book started with Naomi's renewed direction, which led us to examine five purpose-driven questions. Now that we are coming to the end of the story, we must determine to apply those questions to our own lives.

Sometimes we don't need elaborate theological words or concepts—we just need some sound theology the way you might hear it from your grandma: *"God will turn it around!"*

He will, because we can't. For instance, I have spoken with women whom doctors said would never bear a child—yet their kids are now attending school.

And when our acceptance of God's grace changes our eternal status, we must also experience a change in our attitude, our outlook, and our legacy.

I was once skeptical about everything in the gospel. How could I believe the whole world was messed up because two naked people in the woods talked to a snake and ate a piece of fruit? I didn't get it back then, and I understand if you don't get it now.

Regardless, the world is messed up because we humans have wanted to be god of our own lives. Until we sign over the deed of our life to Jesus Christ, we think we are the sole judge and jury of what happens to us. But when we do sign our life over to Him, Jesus changes everything.

God has ways of letting us know He is with us. The change in our eternal status leads to a radical change in our attitude, outlook, and legacy.

Lives of Hope

It's no longer possible to be a "nominal" Christian. "Radical" is the standard, not the exception. When we know our sins have been paid by someone who was perfect, it should lead us to radical faith! Naomi was Jewish and from Bethlehem. We can assume she had faith in God, but when hard times hit her, she wanted to change her name from "pleasant" to "bitter."

Before we judge her, would we have done otherwise? She'd lost her husband and her two sons, and she believed it was God who had caused her to suffer. In fact, as we read earlier, she said the Lord Himself had raised His fist against her (Ruth 1:13).

The thing about tragedy is that it reveals what we value. It reveals the real *us*. Naomi wanted to give up on God, but God wouldn't give up on her. We still see God at work in her life, even when she was making poor decisions. She shouldn't have even been in Moab, but God let her know she could return home.

That's what God does in our lives. He doesn't put a limit on how many times we can come back to Him. God didn't give up on Naomi, either.

In this book, several narratives come together. Naomi was a woman who was supposed to have faith, but she encountered tragedy and her faith was shaken. Ruth was not a believer, but she came to have faith. And God used both her and Boaz to point us to Jesus.

Not only did God use Boaz to redeem Naomi, but He also used their story to help others see His love. In Ruth

4:14, the women of Bethlehem were now talking about Boaz: "Praise the LORD. who has now provided a redeemer for your family!" But some of the characteristics they mentioned are only found perfectly in Christ. In Ruth 4:15, they called Boaz a "restorer of life." He was that, but he restored life only as it related to their need for food and shelter. The true Redeemer, Jesus Christ, restores us so that we can be in right standing with the Father. Boaz could provide for natural needs, but Jesus provides for both natural and supernatural needs.

This means Jesus, as the restorer of life, can redeem our time. No matter how hopeless and broken our lives seem, Jesus will come through for us. Repairing broken lives is His specialty.

Boaz wasn't just a restorer of life. The second thing the women were saying in verse 15 was that Boaz was a "sustainer." This was possible because he was a man of means. But even though he could meet their natural needs, their lives would still end in death.

Anything on this earth in which we put our hope will end in death. Money can be devalued or stolen. Clothing deteriorates and books mildew (though we may hope that this book won't!) while computers crash and cars rust.

As much as we rely on our cars to function properly and transport us safely from place to place, eventually they break down from age—and sometimes prematurely, from accidents. If you don't believe me, ask the deer-shaped dent in my family's Honda! (For the record, the deer hit us, I didn't hit the deer.)

We can't put our faith in possessions. They fade and get dented. We need to put our hope in what is eternal. Jesus is our true nourisher, and He sustains us by giving us undiminished life, with a guarantee of the Holy Spirit. That guarantee is like a deposit that says, "I'm holding you securely."

And the result is a new life with radical faith.

Renewal of Hope

The true Redeemer, Jesus, gives us new life. He tells us in John's Gospel that we must be born again, (John 3:3) and each new life means a renewed legacy. When we turn to Jesus, not everything will be easy, and not everyone will like or love us. In fact, some will reject us because of our new faith. Furthermore, we'll still go through many of the same hardships we faced before being saved.

However, in Christ we have a different response and a renewed perspective. His presence with us, His Spirit in us, and His love for us make all the difference.

In our lives, God will sometimes use someone who doesn't quite fit our bill. They might not look attractive or dress the part, or have much education. He may even use somebody who is poor to provide for us. When God helps us through an unlikely person, we can be sure it's Him.

Look at how God used Ruth in Naomi's story. Naomi was a penniless widow who had lost a husband and two sons. She was poor, in a foreign land, and without food. And how did God provide for her?

Naomi was redeemed because a woman, who was unsaved at the time, said, "Your God will be my God."

Ruth had loved her mother-in-law persistently, even though Naomi had pushed her away. "No," Ruth had said, "wherever you go I will go, wherever you die I will die, and your God will be my God." Her loyalty was all part of God's provision.

God may put us in a situation like Naomi's, where only He can come through—then only He can get the credit.

Are you in a situation where there is no hope? There is a God who can turn the situation around in an instant! God may say, "I want you to be in this helpless, seemingly hopeless situation because right now you are putting your hope in human beings. But if you put your hope in Me, you will have everything you need."

That's how God works. When we realize all we have is Christ, that truth will change our legacy. He is the only one who loves us unconditionally, the only one who doesn't give up on us. Naomi had blown it for ten years, but God kept coming after her.

"If only I could live like that!" you may be saying. The beautiful thing is, you can. You won't do it perfectly, but you *can* live like that.

When Naomi lost hope, God had to remind her that she was never without hope. "I must discipline you sometimes," says God. "You forget who is really in control, so I have to remind you, but I won't give up on you. People might, but I never will."

A Godly Legacy

*Naomi took the baby and cuddled him to her breast. And
she cared for him as if he were her own. The neighbor
women said, "Now at last Naomi has a son again!" And
they named him Obed. He became the father of Jesse and
the grandfather of David.* — **Ruth 4:16-17**

Naomi had a negative attitude at the beginning of the
story. She'd lost her husband and two sons, but what she
had really lost was hope. She had forgotten who was in
control.

In Ruth chapter 1, Naomi had said, in effect, "I don't
have any babies, and I probably won't." Now she was
holding a grandson in her lap! God had come through.
Perception can be dangerous when we limit everything
to the natural.

I wonder what Obed meant to Naomi at this point?
She was probably crying tears of joy. "If only Elimelech
could see me now," she would have thought. "And God,
to think I believed Your hand was against me!"

The answer to her emptiness was a son. The answer to
the *world's* emptiness is a Son. Despite infertility and
every kind of problem, God keeps His promises and in-
stills us with renewed purpose.

The African church father Augustine of Hippo captured this renewing power of God's unconditional love
in his autobiographical work, *Confessions*:

Late have I loved you, beauty so old and so new: late
have I loved you. And see, you were within and I was in

the external world and sought you there, and in my un-lovely state I plunged into those lovely created things which you made. You were with me, and I was not with you. The lovely things kept me far from you, though if they did not have their existence in you, they had no ex-istence at all. You called and cried out loud and shattered my deafness. You were radiant and re-splendent, you put to flight my blindness. You were fragrant, and I drew in my breath and now pant after you. I tasted you, and I feel but hunger and thirst for you. You touched me, and I am set on fire to attain the peace which is yours.[11]

Our motivation for leaving a godly legacy is the beau-tiful reality that God doesn't give up on people, and neither should we. We call it *grace*.

WORKBOOK

Chapter 6 Questions

Question: When you decided to give your life to Jesus, what changed? How does He fill your daily life with purpose?

_____

_____

_____

_____

_____

_____

_____

_____

_____

_____

_____

_____

Question: God can put us in the strangest (and scariest) situations for reasons only He can see clearly at the moment. What is one situation in which God put you, which led Him to get the credit and the glory when you made it through?

_____

_____

_____

_____

_____

_____

_____

_____

_____

_____

_____

Question: What kind of legacy do you want to leave? What are specific ways you can leave a legacy of grace?

_____

_____

_____

_____

_____

_____

_____

_____

_____

_____

_____

Action: Whenever you make a decision, look to God for the wisdom and understanding to see the collateral damage or blessing your choice will create for others. Always choose to be a blessing! Let God use you to manifest His legacy of grace, hope, and love to the lost and the world.

Chapter 6 Notes

CONCLUSION

A Legacy of Love

This is the genealogical record of their ancestor Perez:

Perez was the father of Hezron. Hezron was the father of Ram. Ram was the father of Amminadab. Amminadab was the father of Nahshon. Nahshon was the father of Salmon.

Salmon was the father of Boaz. Boaz was the father of Obed. Obed was the father of Jesse. Jesse was the father of David. **— Ruth 4:18–22**

In the end, Ruth—who began as a stranger to the people of God—assumed her place in the direct earthly lineage of the Son of God.

You will recall how the book of Ruth started during the time of the judges, a period when there was no king and "all the people did whatever seemed right in their own eyes" (Judges 17:6). But it ends with the lineage of David, who would one day become Israel's king.

Moreover, the Gospels trace Jesus' human lineage back through King David to Boaz!

Ruth had come a long way, hadn't she? She was a Moabite outsider, without a heritage of faith in God, and was rejected by Naomi and other women. She had no husband and no child. Now, according to the village women, she was "worth more than seven sons." She had a son of her own and a legacy. From her line the Messiah would come.

For us as heirs of Christ (Romans 8:17), the King has already come. He has entered our situation and promised never to leave us. People may fail us, but if we have hope in Christ, we need never despair.

As we reflect on this story that begins with no king and ends with the announcement that a king is coming, we are reminded that God does not give up on us. He restores our lives and renews our hope for the future. Though He loves us for who we are right now, He loves us too much to let us stay that way.

Therefore, remember Psalm 90:12: "Teach us to realize the brevity of life, so that we may grow in wisdom." Let us consider how our decisions will affect the people around us and the people who will follow us—our children, our spouse, our church, and our community. Instead of thinking only of ourselves, let's live with the end in view.

But there is another side to it: we must, like God, love other people in *this* season of their lives as well. We get frustrated so often because the other person is not who we know he or she could be. But we cannot love someone in a future season. We're to love the person who's with us in *this* one.

This is what it means to love somebody. True love receives the person who's in front of us as he or she is now—and loves the person whom God is shaping him or her to become.

Therefore, love whomever is in front of you now and believe God will continue to work in his or her life. This is what Jesus does in our lives!

We may be works in progress, but God doesn't leave us. He stays with us and loves us into the person He wants us to be. When we embrace this reality, we can live *renewed*.

REFERENCES

Notes

1. Sills, M. David. *Hearts, Heads, and Hands: A Manual for Teaching Others to Teach Others.* B&H Publishing, 2016, p. 394. From "African Impala," *Bible.org.*

2. Saint Athanasius of Alexandria. *On the Incarnation.* Translated by A Religious of C.S.M.V. 1944. Whitaker House, 2016.

3. "Orpah." *Blue Letter Bible.* https://www.blueletterbible.org/search/Dictionary /viewTopic.cfm?topic=ET0002806,HT0001913,I T0006597,NT0003675,BT0003224

4. "What a Diff'rence a Day Makes." Lyrics by Stanley Adams, 1934. Recorded by Dinah Washington, *What a Diff'rence a Day Makes,* 1959.

5. MacDonald, William Graham. From *Baker Encyclopedia of the Bible,* Walter A. Elwell (Ed.). Baker Book House, 1988. In "The Providence of God," *Precept Austin.*

http://www.preceptaustin.org/the_providence_of
_god

6. "2617. checed." *Bible Hub.* Bible Hub.
   http://biblehub.com/hebrew/2617.htm

7. Duguid, Iain. *Esther and Ruth.* P & R Publishing,
   2005.

8. "Love." Lyrics by Musiq Soulchild, 2000. Recorded by Andre Harris and Vidal Davis,
   Aijuswanaseing, 2000.

9. "Just the Way You Are." Lyrics by Bruno Mars,
   Philip Lawrence, Ari Levine, Khalil Walton, &
   Khari Cain, 2010. Recorded by Bruno Mars,
   Doo-Wops & Hooligans, 2010.

10. Smith, Gypsy. In Jonathan Petersen, "You Are
    the Fifth Gospel: An Interview with Bobby Con-
    way." 28 July 2014. *Bible Gateway Blog.* Bible
    Gateway. https://www.biblegateway.com/blog/
    2014/07/you-are-the-fifth-gospel-an-interview-
    with-bobby-conway/

11. Saint Augustine. *The Confessions.* Oxford UP,
    2008, p. 201.

About the Author

Jerome Gay, Jr., is the founder of Vision Church in Raleigh, NC—a gospel-centered, socially conscious, missionally minded, disciple-making church that's serving Raleigh and surrounding areas. At Vision Church, he serves as the Lead Pastor of Teaching, Preaching, and Vision.

Jerome also serves on the board of Thriving, an urban resource collective that equips and trains urban practitioners for ministry and impact. He speaks to churches and organizations all over the country.

He has a Master's Degree in Christian Studies and Ethics from Southeastern Baptist Theological Seminary.

Jerome is married to his lovely wife, Crystal Gay, and is the father of Jamari Christina Gay and Jerome Jordan Gay III.

About Sermon To Book

SermonToBook.com began with a simple belief: that sermons should be touching lives, *not* collecting dust. That's why we turn sermons into high-quality books that are accessible to people all over the globe.

Turning your sermon series into a book exposes more people to God's Word, better equips you for counseling, accelerates future sermon prep, adds credibility to your ministry, and even helps make ends meet during tight times.

John 21:25 tells us that the world itself couldn't contain the books that would be written about the work of Jesus Christ. Our mission is to try anyway. Because in heaven, there will no longer be a need for sermons or books. Our time is now.

If God so leads you, we'd love to work with you on your sermon or sermon series.

Visit www.sermontobook.com to learn more.